new fashion print

print

martin dawber

This book is for Maureen, who introduced me to my first squeegee and
for Charles, an infectious and enthusiastic educator.

To the memory of a great Art School.

First published in the United Kingdom in 2008 by
Batsford
10 Southcombe Street
London
W14 0RA

An imprint of Anova Books Company Ltd

ISBN: 9781906388072

A CIP catalogue record for this book is available from the British Library.

10 9 8 7 6 5 4 3 2 1

Reproduction by Spectrum Colour, Ipswich
Printed and bound by CT Printing Ltd, China
Book design: Lee-May Lim & Mark Holt
Editor: Verity Muir
Cover illustration: *Spiralling Flowers*, Julie Ingham, Helena Gavshon

This book can be ordered direct from the publisher at the website:
www.anovabooks.com

Distributed in the United States and Canada by Sterling Publishing Co., 387
Park Avenue South, New York, NY 10016, USA

illustration (previous page)
design for couture
arthur david

date
2006

media/techniques
collage with textile
fragments/adobe photshop

contents

Foreword

From our birth to our death our bodies are wrapped in cloth. Because of this proximity, textiles are fundamental to all human lives. Many people take their function for granted, but textiles reflect our beliefs, dreams and aspirations. This occurs universally, across the world's cultures.

Contemporary printed textiles have developed into a vehicle for expressing many diverse ideas. Patterns, drawn images, textures, paintings, photographs, and computer-generated imagery can all be seen on the body and in home decoration. Fashion print is a very direct form of communication which has global resonance.

From a historical starting point, imagery in fashion print was strictly limited, for example, it was predominantly paisleys, stripes and florals. Since then the expectation of what printed textiles can be has diversified to include an enormous array of imagery and technique, so that now the range of printed textiles is like that of painting in its variety.

Recent developments in textile technologies have bought us 'intelligent' fabrics that can protect us against pollution and improve our health, heat-sensitive textiles that change colour when touched or alter to accommodate external temperature changes, and ecological textiles made using sustainable sources, including organic materials and recycling.

These changes – in what can be expected of textiles and how they are produced – reflect the way fabrics relate to current cultural values and trends. Fashion print is a very direct way of expressing and reflecting these concerns.

Another great move ahead in textiles is in computer programs and digital printing whereby very sensitive marks and colours and complex computer-generated, layered imagery can be accurately reproduced for the first time.

These developments open up fantastic possibilities for the new generation of textile designers. Imagery has moved on from what could be perceived as 'wearable' ten years ago to an almost unlimited visual vocabulary today. This has resulted in print in fashion being very vibrant and enjoying its return to both couture and the high street.

Fashion designers rely heavily on incredible talents in print, knit, weave, embroidery, embellishment and manipulation. Colour, an essential in fashion, is also the textile designer's forte and responsibility. Despite this, textile designers are the unsung heroes of the fashion industry, unlike designers and models, the majority of fashion print designers are unknown.

I believe this lack of recognition is due for a change and that the wonderful new designers featured here will be names to remember.

This book presents an overview of worldwide contemporary design practice in fashion print featuring 39 international designers representing Europe, USA, Canada, South America, India, Australia and Japan.

One could argue that it has never been a more exciting time to be a fashion print designer.

Helen David
Founder, English Eccentrics

illustration (left)
trellis animals (half drop repeat)
alex russell

date
2005

media/techniques
scanned ink drawings/adobe photoshop

Introduction

Printed textiles have always played an important role within Fashion. The signposts to key moments in 20th-century fashion design are as readily identifiable by the use of images and patterns on fabric as by a single garment's era-defining silhouette. From the organic and elongated decorative shapes that signalled Art Nouveau; via the industrial geometric arrangements that became the insignia of the Constructivists in the 1930s; in the mock-molecular symbols of an emerging 'brave new world' evoking the optimism of the post-War 50s; braving the colour-blocked Pop and Op-art saturation of the 60s & 70s; through to the present-day techno-engineering of Jonathan Saunders and the hedonistic kitsch of Basso & Brooke, printed textiles represent a patterned benchmark by which most of the century's design trends can be tagged.

Erasing environmental issues that bugged design creatives during the 90s, the eve of the millennium saw a welcome exodus from fashion's all-engulfing 'Sea of Black', as print once more took centre stage, unflinchingly elbowing its patterned way down runways across the world and heralding a new decorative era. Not satisfied strutting within the hallowed halls of Paris, Tokyo and New York, the revived look reached out to fashionistas worldwide. From the pervasive fast-fashion bagged at each supermarket sweep, via the global chain-store network, the high street witnessed an unprecedented design explosion, as a riot of pattern and colour infested the urban catwalk. No garment was safe from this invasive pattern-balling attack. Everything from Aussie Bum's retro underwear through to the no-nonsense dressing of Paul Smith, pattern turned up the heat in fashion. No longer a fleeting fad, print resurfaced with such aplomb that it will be difficult to re-bottle this awesomely tattooed genie.

Mirroring similar freedoms in contemporary fashion and global trends, there has been an increase in all types of surface pattern from the tried-and-tested conservative stripe through to organic writhing and complex interlacing. Traditional design stereotypes, such as the ubiquitous florals, inventive geometrics, novelty conversationals, native ethnics and pictorial *toile de jouy* are now being cross-pollinated to create hybrid designs that better reflect today's all-embracing lifestyle. However, not all is multifaceted motifs, there have also been audacious experiments with oversized patterns and shapes – confident, brash, bright and loud and not allowed out since the jumbo geometrics of 70s wallpaper – with bold and stark Marimekkoesque outlines rivalling those retro configurations.

As with most things in the constantly (re)cyclic world of fashion, this re-interest in surface print is freely acknowledged as nothing new. Printed textiles has always borrowed from within itself, as each season, infinite patterns and shapes are skilfully recycled ad infinitum. All patterns have their historical precedent, but as with nature, today's designer has to shape the same information into a new DNA of design. With its easy-to-trace parentage, the task of today's textile designer is to transform their ideas into fresh and innovative surfaces.

Print has always been an essential part of every couturier's bag of tricks. Those worth their golden shears have always been savvy enough to recognise its value and importance.

In the wake of Diaghilev's *Ballets Russes* in 1911, French couturier, Paul Poiret became the first to appreciate and apply this benefit, transferring the oriental patterns designed by Leon Bakst and Alexandre Benois onto his own womenwear collections.

Fauvist painter, Raoul Dufy, who also collaborated with Poiret, is often quoted as saying that 'paintings have spilled from their frames and stained our dress and our walls'. He later embarked on a sixteen-year contract with Bianchini-Férrier that resulted in over 4,000 print designs.

This marriage of the Fine Arts and the consumerist world of fashion was not restricted to France. Liberty's in Britain and the Wiener Werkstatte in Austria were both instrumental in tempting artists to exchange their paints for dyes and help bridge the gap between the *avant-garde* and applied arts. William Morris in London and Gustav Kilmt in Vienna helped to strip away the demarcation lines.

In post-Revolutionary Soviet Union, Constructivist painters, Liubov Popova and Varvara Stepanova, designed their signature abstract and geometric prints at the First State Printed Calico Factory in Moscow. Sonia Delauney transferred her own 'simultanéism' painting style onto printed garments for the couturier, Coco Chanel, while the radical, Elsa Schiaparelli commissioned Surrealists, Salvador Dali and Man Ray.

Unique to this growing cultural exchange were the prints produced by the London fabric workshop founded by Zika and Lida Ascher in 1942. As well as fashioning *haute couture* prints by the metre from artists like Henri Matisse, Feliks Topolski and Henry Moore, they also commissioned printed head squares from an extraordinary roll call of mid-20th-century artists that left most purchasers unsure whether to wear or frame them.

Pop Art became the prevailing characteristic of printed fabrics throughout the 1950s in reaction to the impact of Warhol and Lichtenstein who assigned the mundane iconic status while during the 1960s Art and Fashion remained in close communion through revivals of the decorative floral styles from the Arts and Crafts movement and Art Nouveau. Those design staples now reworked to appeal to a Flower Power generation with purer interpretations of fauna & flora, best symbolised in the simple daisy-head logo designed by Tom Wolsey for Mary Quant.

During the 1980s, Art and Fashion cemented their relationship by the overdue recognition of their alignment at museums in New York, London, Paris and Tokyo.

Since the early 1980s, computer technology has made its impact felt throughout every aspect of printed textiles production – from design through to the manipulation of the print. Digital printing is recognised as the fastest growing system of all available textile printing processes. Its ascendancy is evidenced by its speedy evolution at global textile exhibitions where true digital printing technology made its first impact as recently as 1995 by Stork. Although the textile industry still produces the majority of its billions of square metres output using analog screen-printing methodology, the impact of digital printing has changed the rules of engagement forever, offering faster production and larger cost-effective print runs, promising quality print output at up to 50 metres per hour.

Today's print invasion has knocked design skeptics for six by its spread and speed. Fuelled by the immediacy of new technologies and a 'want-now/buy-now' consumerism, its reappearance has an irresistible dynamism. Challenged by an impatient society fed on a diet of e-communication, today's industry is now able to put the meal on the table in record time. Once the reserve of the elite – today, it is out there for everyone to enjoy.

europe

Laura-Maria Arola

I was born and raised in Finland. The fondest memories I have of my childhood were spending long summer days sat by the lake directly outside my grandmother's house. If I wasn't swimming or exploring the forest, I would be drawing on my dad's computer paper with the newest set of colouring crayons. Still young, we moved to England. This was a hard time for me and I dealt with it by looking through stacks of photographs and drawing countless pictures of home. I've always believed that missing Finland fuelled my creativity and in many ways, it still does.

My passion for art and design took me to London where I studied fashion and textiles at Ravensbourne College of Design and Communication. My eyes were opened to a new direction and my motivation to draw grew. Names such as Marimekko, Eley Kishimoto and Tove Jansson gave me newfound inspiration.

Whilst studying at Ravensbourne, not only did I gain the expertise in various printing methods and fabrics, I learned how to add character and a personal foundation to my work. The crossover between fashion and textiles also proved valuable and I still illustrate my own fashion collections to show where my prints would be used on a garment. I came to realize the importance of knowing how to apply textiles to different areas of design, and saw that it has the potential to push many creative boundaries.

Since I have graduated, I have sold designs to well-known fashion labels, exhibited my work in London and Paris, while my work has been featured in many publications.

My most successful pieces of work have emerged from personal sources. I might extract a certain colour or mood from a photograph or find inspiration in a childhood possession. Drawing an interpretation of what I see, I'd find the strongest features and re-draw them as a separate image, simplifying the shapes and outlines. This process continues until I feel I have found the essence of my original artwork. I use Adobe Photoshop/Illustrator to clean up the image. For the print process, I keep a book packed full of my colour recipes and test fabric swatches. Once I have prepared the recipes and have selected the fabric, my design is ready to be screen-printed.

illustration
waves 01

date
2007

media/techniques
screen print on cotton

Since many of my concepts come directly from experience, the style of my work reflects a personal and nostalgic element. Effective colour combinations and bold silhouettes are a big part of my signature look. My prints have a style that is far from commercial, yet their simplicity allows them to be adapted and applied to a broad range of disciplines.

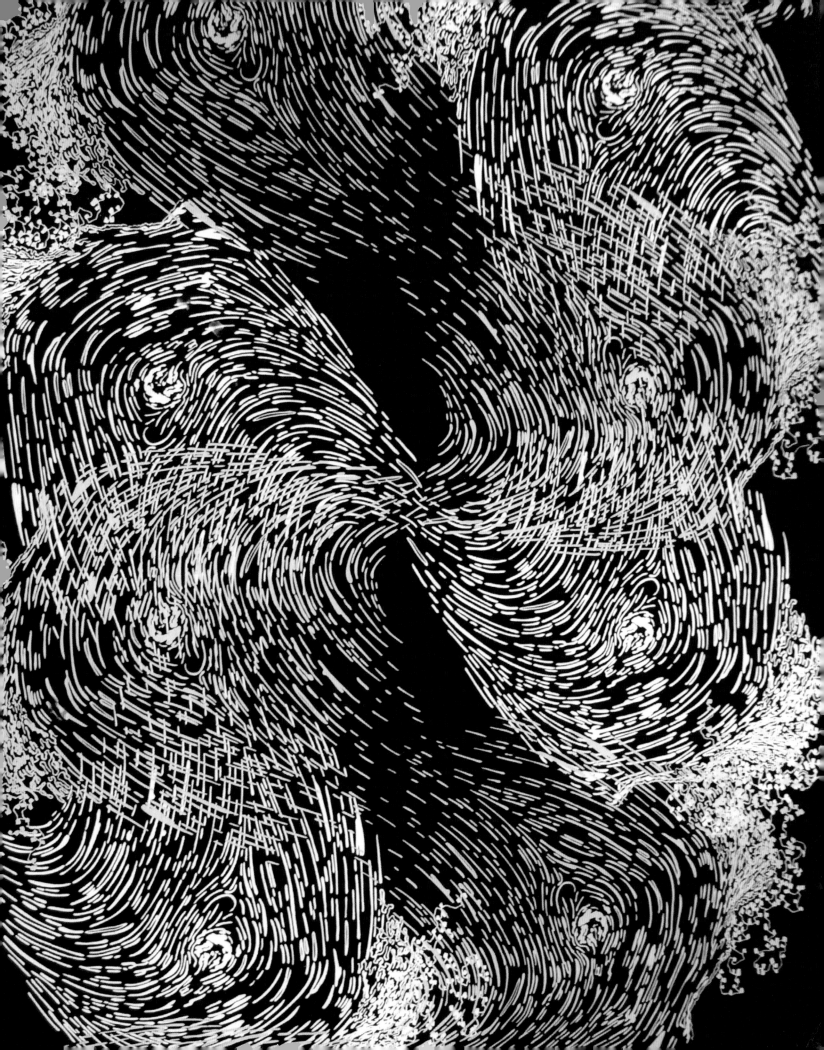

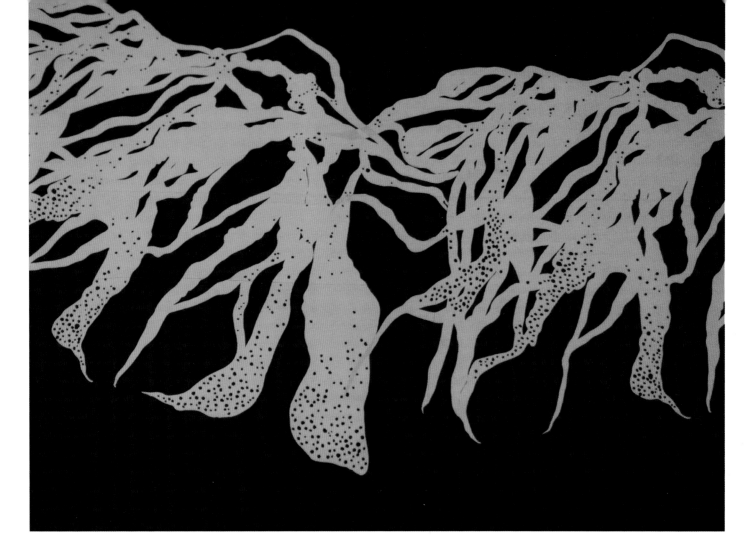

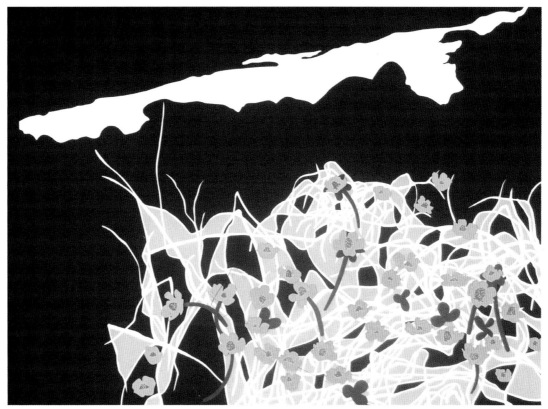

illustration (above)
creature 02

date
2007

media/techniques
screen print on cotton

illustration (right)
spring

date
2007

media/techniques
pen and collaged paper

illustration (above left)
water lilies

date
2007

media/techniques
screen print on cotton

illustration (above)
tall tree 02

date
2007

media/techniques
screen print on cotton

illustration (left)
snowdrops and wood grains

date
2007

media/techniques
screen print on silk-linen

Amsterstampa

We are a print design studio based in Amsterdam that represents the work of 20 designers. The studio was established in 1997 by Frans Verschuren, who operates as both the art director and main sales person.

Each of the artists works in their own very personal way with designs that may vary from computer-generated graphics to hand-painted flowers and many variations in between. It is a unique combination that makes for an exciting mix of styles and handwritings that is constantly evolving. Although most of the designers now live in Amsterdam or elsewhere in the Netherlands, some operate from the US, England and Italy. All the designers work on a freelance basis and some have different jobs. This means that there is a varied amount of influence and information from all over the world pulled together and gathered in our team.

We have regular meetings where we share and pool our information and discuss upcoming trends, ideas and colours. Our collection is very diverse and supplies a wide range of clients, from haute-couture to ready-to-wear, streetwear, sportswear, lingerie, accessories and even swimwear.

We sell our collection in Europe, Japan and the US on regular visits to our clients and we also have a stand at the Indigo Trade Fair in Paris that happens twice a year. We also make designs in response to commissions, especially for

illustration
frans verschuren (designer)

our client's collection.

Our main goal is to make a very contemporary collection with fresh, beautiful

date
2006

and original prints. All will have their own characteristic and fit in with the trends we researched and that our clients want.

media/techniques
feltpen and ink

We believe prints should add fun, character and beauty to the products on which they are they are used.

illustration (above)
bert-jans timmermans
(designer)

date
2007

media/techniques
adobe photoshop

illustration (above right)
(designer) jacqueline
heidanus

date
2006

media/techniques
paper and feltpen

illustration (right)
olivia bertus (designer)

date
2007

media/techniques
feltpen

18

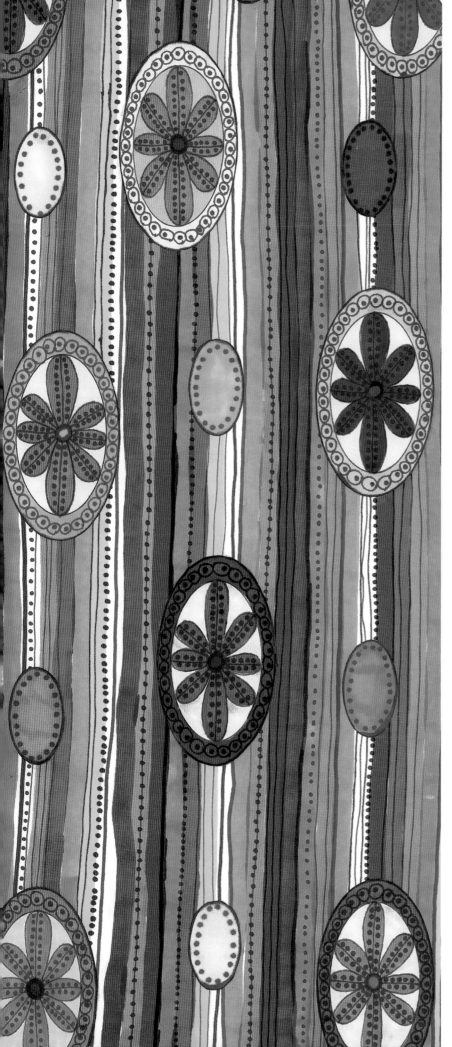

illustration (left)
joos sandbrink (designer)

illustration (above)
stefan jans (designer)

date
2007

date
2007

media/techniques
paper and feltpen

media/techniques
adobe photoshop

19

Giovanna Cellini

I was born and grew up in Rome where I went to school and then to fashion college. I now live and work in London.

Being the daughter of two architects, design has inevitably played a role in my life. I always imagined I was going to be a designer in some way, I think work for me has always meant creating something you can look at.

I didn't train as a textile designer, I studied fashion first and graphic design later in London. Designing textile prints was an almost natural progression: a happy medium between the two.

Although I have an extensive portfolio of prints, I am more of an illustrator with a particular affinity for patterns. I don't really pay attention to market trends nor do I go to trade fairs. The projects I have been involved in have always been on a commission basis where ,following from an initial input from the designer/art director, I develop ideas for prints.

I have been lucky to work for open-minded creative people who are happy to experiment with new ideas rather then conforming to an already-established fashion trend.

All of my prints are put together digitally, using Adobe Illustrator or Photoshop, but I like to start on a project with a more hands-on approach. I often hand draw elements I want to use first, or sometimes I collect or make small objects I can scan in. I find that a handmade element always improves a finished design, adding to it some vitality and vibrancy.

Training in fashion has made me more aware of the end use of my designs. I like to experiment with the placing of the print on the garment and I try to take into consideration the overall look and wearability of the finished product.

illustration
leaves

I think inspiration can come from virtually anything, a conversation with a friend or looking at people and places around me. I look at art, graphic design, fashion and illustration, I am also influenced by music and books. Often an initial idea can change and lead to unexpected and exciting results. I believe it is important to be open-minded and receptive to all sorts of influences.

date
2003

media/techniques
ink/adobe photoshop

Nature is a frequent source of inspiration, with its endless variety of colours and forms. I think I'm spontaneously drawn to organic shapes and fascinated by detail, and all natural forms, from microscopic life to the texture of animal skin. They create an amazing archive of visual reference.

20

illustration (above)	illustration (below)	illustration (below)
arabesco	clouds	arch puzzle (fenchurch clothing)
date	**date**	**date**
2004	2003	2007
media/techniques	**media/techniques**	**media/techniques**
adobe illustrator	ink/adobe photoshop	adobe illustrator

22

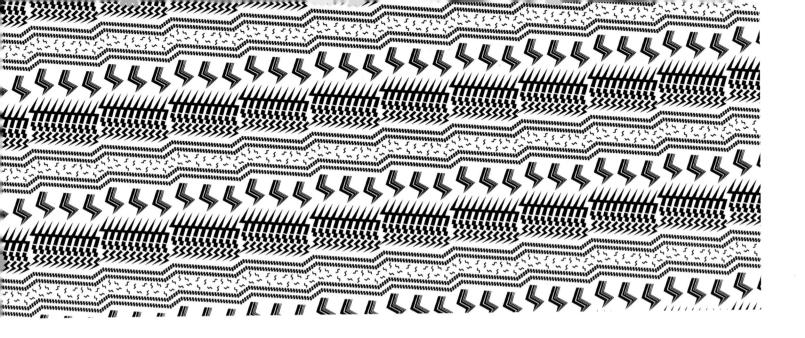

illustration (below)
pigne

date
2006

media/techniques
ink/adobe photoshop

illustration (below)
fans

date
2004

media/techniques
adobe illustrator

illustration (above)
takete (silas)

date
2006

media/techniques
adobe illustrator

Jillian Cole

Having recently graduated with a Degree in Printed Textile Design from Duncan of Jordanstone, I am presently living in the small Scottish Highland town of Pitlochry, surrounded by the hills and mountains of the Perthshire countryside.

The dramatic hills and valleys, rivers and lochs of Perthshire contrast with the gently undulating countryside of Aberdeenshire where I was born and raised. Living so close to the land for most of my life, it is not surprising that both locations have instilled in me an interest in and appreciation of nature and landform, be it the vivid contrasting colours and grandeur of Perthshire, or the expansive views of Aberdeenshire, where each fold in the landscape reveals a different hue and texture.

In my childhood I enjoyed drawing and painting so that on attending Ellon Academy, my secondary school, I chose art as one of my main subjects, which allowed my interest to develop and mature. I was given much encouragement by the school's art department where I learned to question how things took a particular form or what the intentions of a design were. Evaluating the good aspects of a design together with the flaws, how materials and colours were chosen and combined were all part of this questioning process.

Having such close contact to nature has resulted in much of the inspiration for my work being drawn from natural flora, be it cultivated or from the wild. A high proportion of my work originates from hand drawings and sketches of plant life, and also photographic images of flowers and foliage. I particularly enjoy combining detailed and complex line drawings with spots of intense colour. My design process may also involve the manipulation of my drawings or other images on the computer, to produce finished designs, suitable for digital printing on fabrics such as cotton and silk. Although many of my designs are in repeat form, I also like to work with non-repeating designs.

While the basis of much of my design work exploits the natural beauty and shape found in nature, I also like to incorporate geometric forms such as lines, grids and circles, sometimes by way of contrast, but also to provide a structure for the design on which the organic forms can intertwine and be supported.

illustration
free fall

date
2007

media/techniques
adobe photoshop

I create designs for both fashion fabrics and interiors, but it is the fashion possibilities about which I am most enthusiastic. When creating a new design for fabric, I generally will have an end use in mind from the outset, be it for a dress or an accessory. I will also aim to have a design for the dress or accessory in mind, so that the final design is as appropriate for the intended item as I can make it.

24

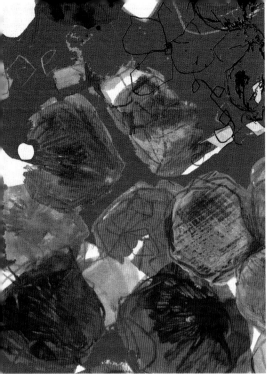
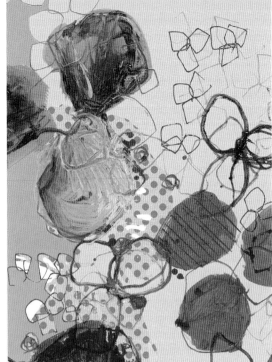

illustration (above)
hot crêpe

date
2007

media/techniques
adobe photoshop

illustration (above centre)
custard creme

date
2007

media/techniques
adobe photoshop

illustration (above right)
lemon leaf

date
2007

media/techniques
adobe photoshop

illustration (opposite left)
violets

date
2007

media/techniques
adobe photoshop

illustration (right)
card sharp

date
2007

media/techniques
adobe photoshop

Arthur David

I was born and currently work in Zurich, Switzerland. As a child, I wanted to become concert pianist and conductor. Later I discovered wonderful books about Le Corbusier, Mies van der Rohe, Frank Lloyd Wright and Jean Prouvé. These and others created my initial ignition towards the visual sphere. Today, art and music are always important for my work.

I respond to the creativity needed for printed textiles and approve that technical obstacles in its production and manufacture do not limit its design. For me, the proportions of the human body become the creative experiment field. I like interesting and inspiring humans taking the motivation for my designs from today's urban environments, the street, culture and civilized races.

Important sources of influence are both the contemporary art and music scene as well as African culture. Also I find the artistic ambivalences of the 1920s and 1930s very interesting. In the world of art I admire the work of Francis Bacon, Cy Twombly, Barnett Newman and Bruce Nauman. In fashion I really like Rei Kawakubo, Issey Miyake, Junya Watanabe and Vivienne Westwood. I like the mixture between contemporary expression and tradition; between purism and sumptuousness.

I prefer bouts of spontaneity followed by reflection before I realize my designs. I think graphic and abstract designs work best. I work directly with drawing, painting, paper cuts and photographic material before transferring across to the computer. My first designs develop from these varied puzzle components.

Although repetition can be aesthetically interesting I prefer to design on panneau size without being restricted by repetition. Using today's digital technology, it is now possible to print directly and precisely onto the shape of the garment. I really like the new textile materials, for example the metallic fabrics or fluorescent paillettes for printing.

illustration
design for the couture 6

date
2006

media/techniques
crumpled pages of a lifestyle
magazine/adobe photoshop

Although each designer must recognize current trends and styles they also need to be extremely playful in their response. The look and the feeling of the work is crucial.

Today's designers need to have a burning passion for fabrics and also a really good understanding of fashion. I would encourage all new students to make the addition of a second area of study: fashion, graphic design or photography. This will expand their view and prevent the focus on just pure textiles.

28

illustration
design for the couture
– collection 'arthur david'

date
2005

media/techniques
digital/transfer print on
polyester (manufactured by
jakob schlaepfer,
switzerland)

31

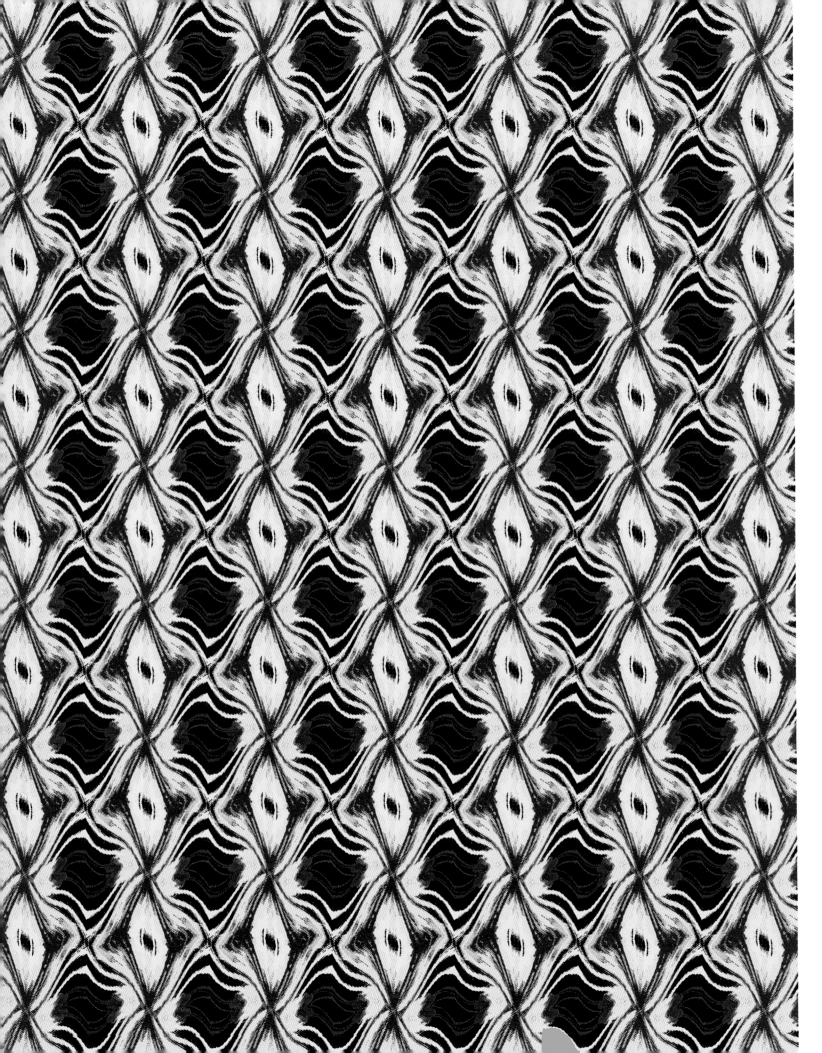

illustration (opposite)
design for ready-to-wear 1

date
2006

media/techniques
drawing/adobe photoshop

illustration (below)
design for the couture 9

date
2005

media/techniques
collage/adobe photoshop

illustration (below)
design for the couture 2a

date
2005

media/techniques
collage/adobe photoshop

Vicki Fong

I completed my BA in Fashion Textiles with Business Studies at Brighton University before graduating from London's Royal College of Art with an MA in Printed Textiles.

I was born in Yorkshire to Chinese parents. My two cultures resulted in some very interesting conversations in the school playground and, although I learnt to keep quiet about the bird phlegm soup, there was no escaping the more vociferous rituals: a new house not only involved removal vans and DIY, it also meant Feng Shui readings, sacrificial chickens, and the explosion of a thousand lucky firecrackers.

It is these very Chinese customs that have provided the inspiration for my work. Using illustrations and collaged images, I have explored the crossover between Eastern traditions and Western aesthetics.

To this day, my work always begins with a narrative. My portfolio is inspired by unusual perspectives, such as the pigeons' victorious invasion of London and the beauty of decaying fish. These ideas are translated through a broad array of media: ranging from ink pens to oil paints and photography to collage.

I love mixing traditional skills with the more modern methods afforded by computers and digital printers. Digital technology has helped me master repeats more effectively and provides me with an endless capacity for colour and scale. I use these techniques to apply my designs on to different surfaces: from everyday fashion and interiors to gallery installation pieces.

On an industry level, I expect that digital technology – with its benefits of affordability, a near-limitless colour palette, the ability to print on demand, and its environmentally neutral status – will continue to be the key driver. Its user-friendly accessibility allows designers from non-textile backgrounds to become involved, thereby enriching and expanding the scope of the medium.

illustration
chicken broth

date
2006

media/techniques
pen, paper, adobe
photoshop

I now live and work in London. I frequently exhibit in galleries as well as freelance design. Recently, this included a print commission for the Spring/Summer 2007 collection for the British fashion label, Modernist.

My second passion is music and I find motivation in the techno beats of Dave Clarke, the quirky electro vocals of The Knife, and the rich cultural sounds of M.I.A. I also take inspiration from gallery visits, my interest in comics, and my own life experiences. I am always grateful for the support provided by my family, friends and tutors – all have helped me to get to where I am today.

illustration (above)
hydrate

date
2006

media/techniques
gouache,
adobe photoshop

illustration (above right)
bird nest soup

date
2006

media/techniques
gouache,
adobe photoshop

illustration (right)
unlucky fish

date
2006

media/techniques
pen/adobe photoshop

illustration (left)	**illustration (above)**
feathers	lucky coins
date	**date**
2006	2006
media/techniques	**media/techniques**
gouache, adobe photoshop	ink, adobe photoshop

Nadja Girod

The patterns I make are often described as quirky, funny and naïve. They certainly fit Berlin, the city where I was born, grew up in, and still enjoy living in. The fashion changes here like anywhere else, but it's a place with a strong desire to escape the mainstream, where eccentricity and the offbeat thrive and are constantly sought after. It is also a city that's fun to live in and is alive with new ideas. It certainly has helped shape both me and my work.

At a very early age I remember a brief period of wanting to be an airline stewardess, like everyone else in my class. However, this period was soon to pass, and I decided to become a fashion designer instead. I later studied pattern drafting and fashion design at Esmod Berlin. Early on in my career I experimented with many different forms of design, which I still occasionally enjoy doing, but it was during an internship at H&M that I first discovered my greatest design passion: that of creating patterns for textiles. It is this which gives me my greatest design buzz.

I can't really put into words why that's so, but I think I have a good eye for patterns and enjoy putting that ability to work in creating new ideas.

It is especially satisfying when I have a project that I initially believe is a little beyond my grasp: I believe this helps me grow as a designer and helps keep the designs fresh too.

I love all-over prints and repeats. I think good things should be repeated. Every pattern is a world in itself with its own underlying rules. The interaction of concept, colours and level of abstraction is essential for a good print. When working for a client there are usually many restrictions, which can be a little frustrating at times. Communication is the key to understanding the client's needs and helps in the designing of a good print.

One designer whose work I greatly admire is Graziela Preiser. She did some pretty amazing prints for bedding in the 70s that have since turned into design classics. I'm dreaming of designing prints as timeless as hers.

illustration
shades

date
2007

media/techniques
macromedia freehand

Inspiration can be found anywhere: a line of a song stuck in my head; shadows of trees on the wall; something I find in a flea market, and so on. If I see anything interesting, I take a picture and put it in my sketchbook. Over the years I have filled up many sketchbooks. I now only wish that I had more time to transform these ideas into prints.

illustration (below)
herbarium

illustration (right)
clamberer

date
2005

date
2007

media/techniques
macromedia freehand

media/techniques
macromedia freehand

illustration (above)
what dogs want

date
2006

media/techniques
macromedia freehand

illustration (below)
russian dancer

date
2007

media/techniques
macromedia freehand

illustration (below)
tennis anyone?

date
2007

media/techniques
adobe photoshop

Julie Ingham

I grew up in Hull, East Yorkshire. I was always interested in textiles and art; winning local painting competitions as a child. My parents bought me a second-hand Singer sewing machine and I spent many happy hours making rags dolls and dressing them. My education took the normal course: A levels, Foundation in Art and Design. This was followed by a BA Degree in Textile design at Bretton Hall College and then a PGDIP in Textiles at Leeds University.

For the past 15 years I have had studios in central London. However, since I am expecting twins, my husband and I have moved out to the seaside town of Worthing in West Sussex and I am currently working from a studio at home.

My inspiration comes from anything visual – from a painting to a door knob. I am constantly looking at things and am really surprised when other people don't see what I see.

I love to play and to work with many techniques. Sadly the invention of CAD means that most things I work on today are designed on the computer and I don't play with materials as much as I used to. Adobe Photoshop is the main software program I use; it's very flexible, and allows me to develop things by hand, which can be scanned in, as well as designing directly with the program.

I love designing patterns for objects from fashion to tableware and working with them every day. However, whilst I really love pattern, I tend to buy for myself objects and clothes with plain block colours or very simple patterning.

Favourite art includes David Hockney's new large landscape paintings of Yorkshire; Joceyln Warner's wallpapers; Orla Kiely's pattern sense; Picasso's ceramics. I also love the vintage designs of the 1920s, 1930s and 1950s.

I like to visit the Indigo print fair in Paris where my work is often displayed and I visit Ambiente in Frankfurt too. I also love to visit shows such as Origin and 100% Design as you see much more innovative design there.

illustration
geometric leaves (number 3)
helena gavshon

I hope the future is a much greener one; sadly I am not sure this will happen. Cheap labour is often used as well as chemicals that are highly damaging to the environment. Designers are not always very highly paid but the consumer continues to consume and wants products that are very inexpensive.

date
2006

To students considering entering this fascinating world of pattern I would say enjoy what you are doing and do it because you want to. Above all, designing takes passion and commitment.

media/techniques
adobe photoshop

illustration (right)
hydranger (number 14)
helena gavshon

date
2007

media/techniques
adobe photoshop

illustration (below left)
flowers and checks (number 5)
helena gavshon

date
2006

media/techniques
adobe photoshop

illustration (below right)
floral geometric (number 6)
helena gavshon

date
2005

media/techniques
adobe photoshop

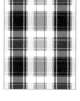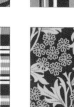

illustration (far left)
red flowers (number 11)
helena gavshon

date
2007

media/techniques
adobe photoshop

illustration (left)
dancing Flowers (number 8)
helena gavshon

date
2006

media/technique
adobe photoshop

illustration (far left)
oriental flowers (number 15)
helena gavshon

date
2006

media/techniques
adobe photoshop

illustration (left)
little pink flowers (number 4)
helena gavshon

date
2006

media/techniques
adobe photoshop

James Francis Millar

I am originally from a small town outside Glasgow, and obtained a degree in Printed Textiles from Glasgow School of Art before moving to London to complete an MA in fashion at Central Saint Martins, focusing on print for fashion.

I always wanted to pursue a creative career but only really fell into textiles over time and upon the recommendations of teachers at high school. I knew nothing about the medium at that time but during the course of my degree research I became more interested in the use of print within fashion.

A love of drawing meant that print was a natural extension for me due to the image-based nature of the medium. I love the immediacy of print, you can see instant results and therefore react/redesign as you go along. It's much more evolving as a process than say constructed textiles. This makes print more similar to the process of creating art, though I do not consider it art.

Inspirations are eclectic and wide-ranging, encompassing music, art, magazines and fashion. In particular I am inspired by Jean Paul Goude (art director), Janine Janet (sculptor), the fashion/style of David Bowie and Prince, the fashion design of Geoffrey Beene and Issey Miyake, and the art of Franz Kline and Sam Francis.

I love to combine new and old, sometimes using old prints as inspiration, using digital printing techniques in combination with traditional screen printing processes. In particular I like to bleach prints in areas to create a more 'honest' feel to create a unique and individual surface.

Often I am inspired by collage and thus create prints that appear to repeat but in fact do not. I tend to lean towards this approach with placement prints applied on top, mixing medias.

I work for a studio part-time where all the prints are done by hand with a strong emphasis on drawing. This work is sold at private sales appointments and at major trade fairs around the world by the studios sales team. The rest of the time I do my own work, which is usually computer-based. This work is made into final garments that I sell through a store in Japan and so I often have to consider the final application rather than creating 'running yardage'.

I don't see textiles heading for any particular future. As technology changes so will processes but there is always going to be the desire for the hand-crafted approach as it is more aesthetically pleasing. Therefore I would recommend gaining knowledge in both these areas as a good way to move the design process forward and create new and interesting textiles.

illustration
tulip (section of ss08)

date
2007

media/techniques
adobe photoshop

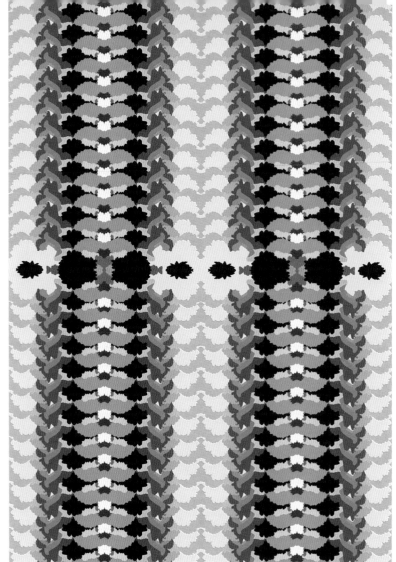

illustration (above)

goude

date

2005

media/techniques

adobe photoshop

illustration (above right)

gypsy

date

2005

media/techniques

adobe photoshop

illustration (right)

martin

date

2005

media/techniques

adobe photoshop

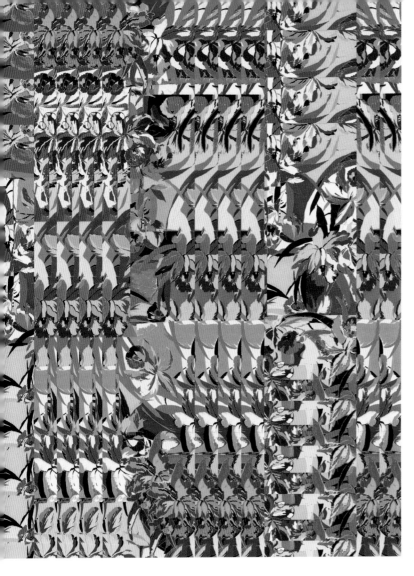

illustration (left)
section of ss08 tartan print

date
2007

media/techniques
adobe photoshop

illustration (below left)
section of 'deer' print for
nicola de main
date
2007

media/techniques
adobe photoshop

illustration (below)
baker

date
2005

media/techniques
adobe photoshop

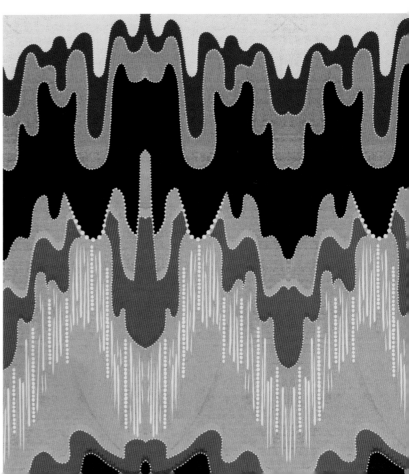

Rupert Newman

I grew up in Devon and went to Sherborne School in Dorset, where I was encouraged to develop my own distinctive personal style while studying an art movement called Rayonism, a Russian movement in the early 1900s where the artists painted the light rays reflected from objects rather than the objects themselves. So from the start, my artwork has had a kaleidoscopic resonance.

At University College Falmouth I experimented with my own mono-print techniques, and discovered how to repeat the original motif with a roller. This led me to produce a collection of wallpaper designs, following which I focused my creative ambitions into the world of textile design using the digital print facilities at Falmouth.

My design process begins with building up mono-print imagery in my sketchbook. I draw, paint and collage over these skeletal images. I work with each piece again, carefully creating layers with hard edges of colour, and achieving 3-dimensional depth on a 2-dimensional surface. Designing in this way allows for structure, and the structure of colour and shape creates a balanced harmony on the page.

I am always mindful that the work produced will be scanned into the computer and repeated for textile application. After scanning into Photoshop, I tidy the images and then reconstruct the edges so the original motif will allow for half-drop repeat. I have developed other techniques on Photoshop to create varied collections, such as circular patterns and animalistic abstractions.

My style has been influenced by many artists. Mikhail Larionov, Lyonel Feininger and Robert Delaunay have inspired me to paint fractured light. Sonia Delaunay especially influenced me with her emphasis on applying art to craft. Cubism, Suprematism and Orphism are some of the movements that I am interested in, as they are concerned with, as I am, juxtaposed colour, and re-organizing space in composition.

illustration
architectural repeat

date
2006

media/techniques
mono print/adobe
photoshop/digital print on
cotton canvas

My lifestyle in the sunny South West has also influenced my work – the motion of the waves and surf, the crystal clear light and the rhythms of my African Djembe are reflected in some of my most vibrant abstract compositions. I believe modern abstract textile design should reflect these characteristics, as an alternative to more traditional 'flowery' patterns.

I have successfully shown my collections in London (First View) and Paris (Indigo-Premier Vision) after receiving a prestigious award. My work has been sold worldwide for fashion and interior fabric, as well as for decorative display.

50

illustration (above)
colliding prism

date
2006

media/techniques
paint/adobe photoshop/
digital print on linen

illustration (above top)
cow division

date
2005

media/techniques
paint/adobe photoshop/
digital print on cotton canvas

illustration (above)
crystal explosion

date
2006

media/techniques
paint/adobe photoshop/
digital print on cotton canvas

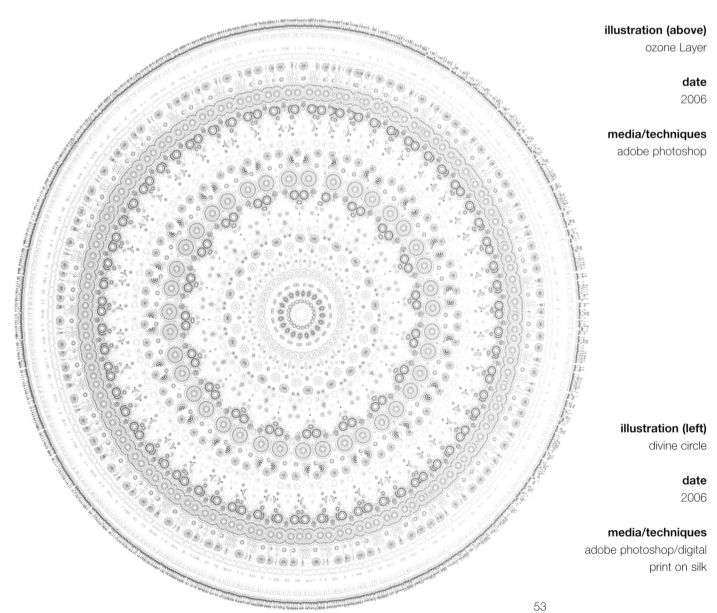

illustration (above)
ozone Layer

date
2006

media/techniques
adobe photoshop

illustration (left)
divine circle

date
2006

media/techniques
adobe photoshop/digital
print on silk

Nathalie Pellon

I grew up in France and Switzerland. My childhood was full of dreams and fantasy worlds. In school I often looked out of the window, day-dreaming. I used to play 'circus' with my friends — charmed by the glittery glamour world of the artists. I was just nine years old when I created costumes for the first time, out of old sheets and sequins and beads. This was a defining moment for my future career as a designer.

I first trained as an arts and crafts teacher. In my early twenties I enjoyed animating children to find their creative potential. For a long time I wasn't sure if I should take the path of fashion or textile design. After a brief start in fashion I decided to study textile design. I love to play with colours and forms and I enjoy seeing the fabrics adjust through movement. I see myself as a designer and not as an artist. My work has always sat in-between art and craft.

The history of fashion is a great source of inspiration but visiting all kinds of exhibitions encourages my thoughts to wander and helps me to create new designs. I think, as a designer, I'm always receptive. I believe that everything can be inspiration; a movie, nature or even just a feeling. In fact life itself is full of inspiration. I really love playing with colours – how the same pattern looks completely different in various colours. The statement can absolutely change – colours are my playground.

My method of approach has been strongly influenced by my internship in a forecast agency in Paris. It's rather a conceptual thing. I do a lot of research for a particular theme, create a matching colour palette, make a mood board and give titles before I design patterns. The research part often opens up new worlds – unseen colours or astonishing forms, in my own vocabulary of design.

My designs are mostly hand-drawn and inspired by traditional patterns, photographs or geometrical figures. I scan the drawings and then I arrange them into the final pattern using Adobe Photoshop. In doing so I have the possibility to play very quickly with repeats, dimensions, density and colours –

illustration
circles

until I like the result. Sometimes this happens very fast, other times I rearrange and rearrange and – rearrange again! I then print the design and take a look at it from some distance to see if it still works.

date
2005

I now live in Berne and work from my studio in an old factory and, since I have become a mother, often at home. I do freelance work as a costume designer for various dance companies, as a trend consultant for varying firms and I

media/techniques
hand drawing/adobe
photoshop

design patterns for different projects. I also enjoy working part-time as a university lecturer for textile crafts at the teacher-training college in Berne.

54

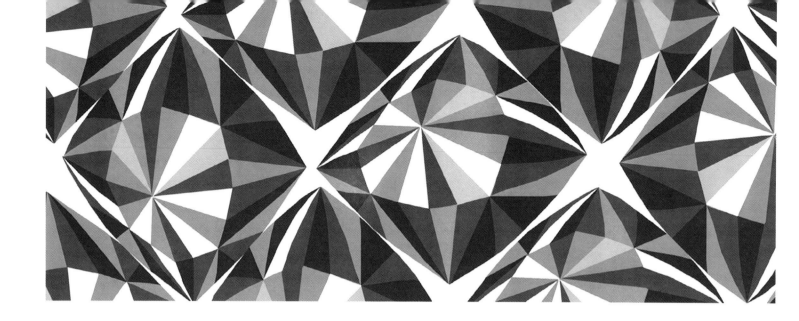

illustration (above)
diamond

date
2003

media/techniques
hand drawing/adobe
photoshop

illustration (right)
origami

date
2002

media/techniques
hand drawing/adobe
photoshop/point carre

illustration (right)
summer

date
2005

media/techniques
hand drawing/adobe
photoshop

illustration (left)
spiro

date
2005

media/techniques
hand drawing/adobe
photoshop

illustration (above)
winter

date
2006

media/techniques
hand drawing/adobe
photoshop

Gina Pipét

After studying Fine Art and Textiles at College, I went on to university to specialise in Printed Textiles, graduating from Winchester School of Art in England. I moved to north London shortly after, and I currently work full time for Liberty of London Design studio. When not at work, I spend any free time I have establishing my own style, creating elaborate and decorative patterns, and expanding my design portfolio from my studio at home.

I have always been influenced by graphic art and drawing, and find the works of M.C Escher and Victor Vasarely fascinating in their use of perception and illusion to create the most intriguing works. I admire the decorative beauty in the work of artists and designers such as Mucha, Morris and Voysey, and find inspiration from the lines and forms in sculpture from artists such as Hepworth and Moore.

My drawings often interpret the construction of everyday items, with the components they are made from often being as interesting as the object itself. For me, designing is about the viewer appreciating the image, considering and deciphering its content rather than just taking it at face value.

At university I specialised in screen printing on fabrics, papers and vinyl, experimenting with various finishes and techniques. More recently I work in digital media as it allows me to develop my designs further, experimenting more freely with the use of colour, scale, and repeat which would otherwise not be possible. CAD also enables me to visualise and present my work extremely well.

When creating my patterns I start with a collection of sketches, which develop into a series of starting points for my designs. I try not to have a fixed, preconceived idea of the end use of my design, as I feel this can be quite restricting. Designing a pattern is a process which the end use should be allowed to alter, becoming more apparent as the image develops, applying it to various items other than that initially thought.

illustration
mae fleur 2

It is essential to consider market trends and current fashions but I think it is important to use these as a guide only. I visit trade fairs for work and see this as an important way to keep yourself up to date with current fashions and trends of the companies around you.

date
2007

I think prints in fashion should be braver. Designers should not be scared to create more daring and exciting prints, using them in such a way which compliments a collection rather than overwhelming it. I would like to see print being applied to a wider variety of surfaces, experimenting with base materials, textures and finishes that enhance the item it is applied to.

media/techniques
hand drawing/adobe
photoshop

58

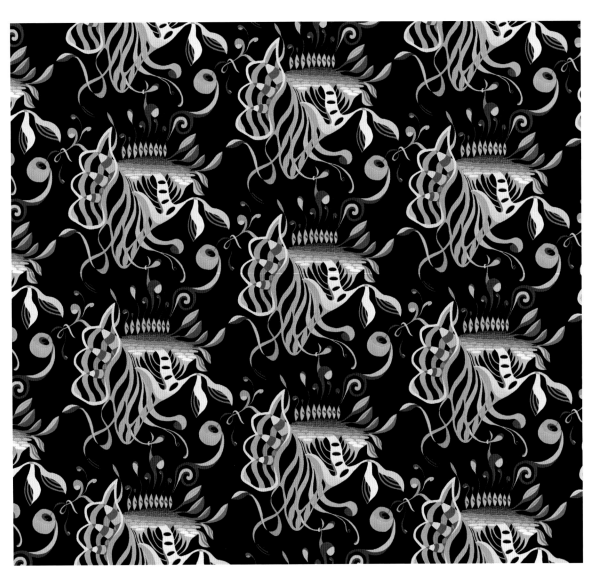

illustration (above)

concee

date

2007

media/techniques

hand drawing/adobe
photoshop

illustration (above right)

bamboo water

date

2007

media/techniques

hand drawing/adobe
photoshop

illustration (right)

umpala

date

2005/7

media/techniques

hand drawing/adobe
photoshop

60

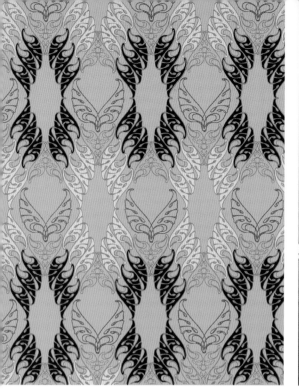

illustration (above left)
herais

date
2007

media/techniques
adobe photoshop

illustration (above)
chane

date
2007

media/techniques
hand drawing/adobe
photoshop

illustration (left)
rohe 2

date
2007

media/techniques
adobe photoshop

Alex Russell

I grew up in Dorset, studied in Manchester, before lecturing in Nottingham, then designing in Brussels and Amsterdam. Now I live and design in Leicester and lecture at Manchester Metropolitan University. I run a studio called Alex Russell Creative Services, specialising in printed textile design, surface pattern, fashion graphics and illustration.

It wasn't until I was nearly 20 that I entertained the thought of a design career. I'd started a degree in electronic engineering but hated it, so left and did an art foundation. I'd been screen printing since my early teens and had always been intrigued by pattern. Choosing printed textiles felt very natural. What I do isn't art or craft, it's design. I'm not entirely sure what that means, but it isn't something that forces us to re-examine the way we think about notions of the subject on any number of different levels. If you asked me what turned me on as a designer, I'd say unpopular culture.

My inspirations are:
• Things that look like nothing I've ever seen before.
• Things that look like everything I've ever seen before.
• Things I wish I'd thought of.
• Things that make me want to work out why they caught my eye.

The creative process always starts with pencil and paper and always ends with a full-scale design. What happens in between varies wildly, although I generally work on collections of designs simultaneously. End use is a vital consideration, never a restriction.

I think it's really important to know what's going on in terms of market trends, not least because it inspires confidence in potential clients. To what degree you choose to be influenced by trends is up to you or your brief.

illustration
blumen half tone (half drop repeat)

date
2006

media/techniques
digital photography/adobe photoshop

My suggestions to people thinking of becoming printed textile designers:
• Work very hard. Be very patient.
• Answer the brief. Answer it on time.
• Get your work out there.
• Constantly chase up leads and seek new contacts.
• Never mess with copyright.
• Always work on new ideas.
• Colour is vital. So is drawing.
• Do really good work. Have fun doing it.
• Never reveal all your secrets.

illustration (previous page)
rough vector cala lily
(half drop repeat)

date
2006

media/techniques
digital photography/adobe
photoshop/adobe illustrator

illustration (below)
transparent flower spheres
(half drop repeat)

date
2006

media/techniques
adobe illustrator/adobe
photoshop

illustration (below)
giant poppies
(half drop repeat)

date
2007

media/techniques
scanned paintings and
drawings/adobe photoshop

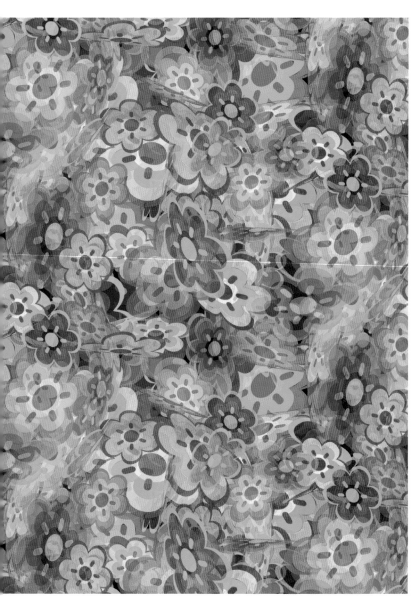

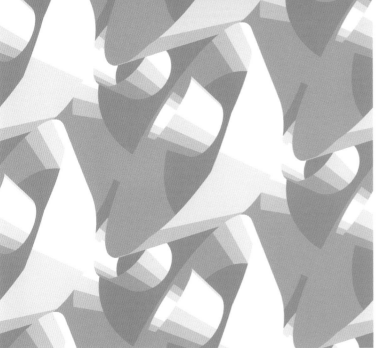

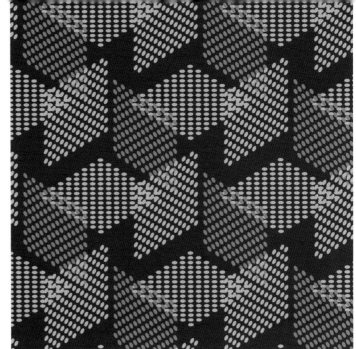

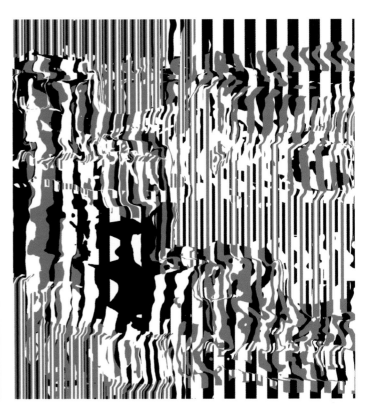

illustration (top left)

3D speaker stack (half drop repeat)

date

2006

media/techniques

adobe illustrator/adobe photoshop

illustration (above)

hot dot tempo (half drop repeat)

date

2004

media/techniques

ink drawings/digital photography/adobe photoshop

illustration (top right)

clean dot grid (block repeat)

date

2007

media/techniques

adobe illustrator/adobe photoshop

illustration (above)

displaced stripe three (half drop repeat)

date

2005

media/techniques

adobe photoshop

Niamh Smith

I recently graduated from the National College of Art and Design, Dublin with a Bachelor of Art in Printed Textile design. I had a keen interest in art from a very young age and have always been highly inspired by the beautiful Irish countryside in which I grew up. My mother, who is also an artist has been a huge influence and guide in my career. During my time in college I completed a work placement at London's exciting textile studio 'Circleline design'. This greatly influenced my final degree show work and made me realise that I was interested in creating textiles using innovative new processes. On leaving university, Circleline then offered me a full time job so I moved to London.

In the studio I create fun and exciting prints for various markets worldwide, from high-street to high-end, furnishing to advertisement, with an emphasis on being different. My inspiration comes from everywhere, I am constantly on the look out for new ideas, I often find that visiting current exhibitions and galleries boosts my imagination further. I am very visually aware and can find inspiration in the strangest places. In 2006 I took a year out to travel the world and got hugely inspired by the amazing variety of textiles throughout the countries I visited. I collected and sourced fabrics and references from India, South-East Asia, Indonesia and South America, which I have used in my designs since returning.

I am also a keen photographer and have found this is a useful source of inspiration towards design work.

The discipline required to design printed textiles means expressing my creativity and been completely open-minded. I like coming up with something different, being experimental and pushing the boundaries. I would describe my work as spontaneous, fresh, colourful with an emphasis on the avante garde. I like to have diversity in my work. When designing it is important to consider the season you are designing for. Colour, imagery, scale and fabric type all play an important part in this. I find that working on the computer gives me more control.

illustration
psychedelic symmetry

With regards to trends, I like to predict and not follow, to be one step ahead, but it is also important to be aware of the trends to cater for the more commercial market. I travel to trade fairs in Paris twice annually and New York once annually with Circle-line, here I find that it is really beneficial to meet clients and see their reaction to my work.

date
2007

media/techniques
adobe photoshop

In the ever-increasing world of fashion and textiles, the only way forward is to make your mark with an individual statement.

68

illustration
pearly queen

date
2006

media/techniques
adobe photoshop

illustration
ditsystitch

date
2006

media/techniques
adobe photoshop

illustration
pretty petal polka

date
2007

media/techniques
adobe photoshop

illustration
bejewelled

date
2007

media/techniques
adobe photoshop

americas

Claudette Carino

Although I now live and work from my studio in Brooklyn, New York, I grew up in a small town in Ohio. Until I left, I relied on my dad's subscription to *National Geographic* as an escape to the outside world. As a result, I was exposed to all the beautiful patterns and textiles that were being designed.

I eventually decided to attend the Rhode Island School of Design as a painting major. From there I went on to paint murals in Boston and Chicago, before returning to the Fashion Institute of Technology in New York.

Any type of creativity to me is in itself an art. I take inspiration from everything – art, other types of design, nature, everything really. For me there is a pattern to all aspects of life and I really love green design. It's so innovative and creative. I love the idea of great design being accessible and serving a purpose. I have always loved Beatriz Milhazes, an amazing Brazilian artist.

At the moment I really like graphic designers. There is just so much amazing work out on the web right now and I am always really inspired by what I see.

When designing a print it is really important to ask who and what it is for. Once I have established an idea, I will either take my sketches and scan them onto my computer and create from there or just continue the sketch into a painting. Everything that I work on has my personal twist. I just love to create and for me it is a continuous process.

In terms of selling designs, it's very important to consider market trends, but considering how fast everything moves today, this can be difficult. With the advent of H&M and similar stores, the turnover from idea to design to production is very rapid. In this respect I find that is a good idea to always know what is going on in all aspects of art and design, and try to translate those trends into a design immediately. It is always good to visit trade fairs to see what is out there for both inspiration and to see what your competition is!

illustration
cherries

I think the evolution in printed textiles will be in the material and manufacturing; greener and different types of processes. I think we'll see more print design in industrial fabrics, such as luggage, outerwear fabrics, etc.

date
2007

media/techniques
adobe illustrator

I feel that it is very important for new designers to learn current computer programs. Coming from a Fine Art background and being a little resistant to new technology, I am grateful that I learned to use the programs that have since become an integral part of textile design. My motto is just love what you do and you'll be fine.

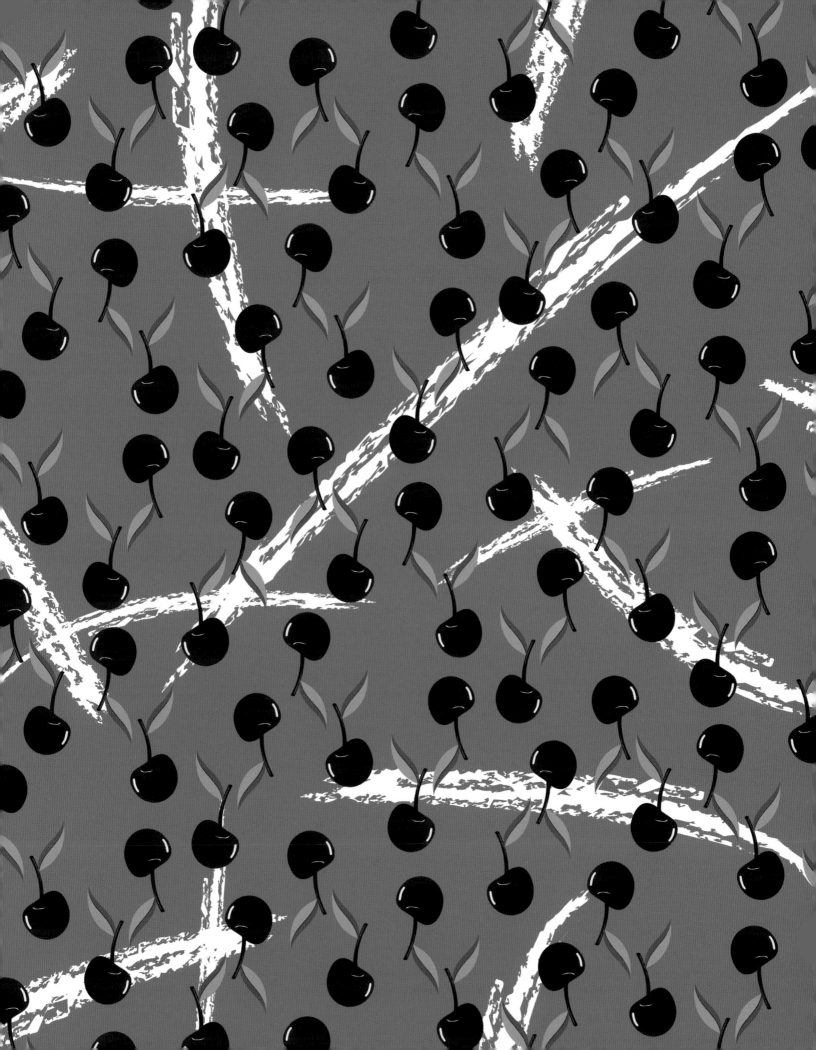

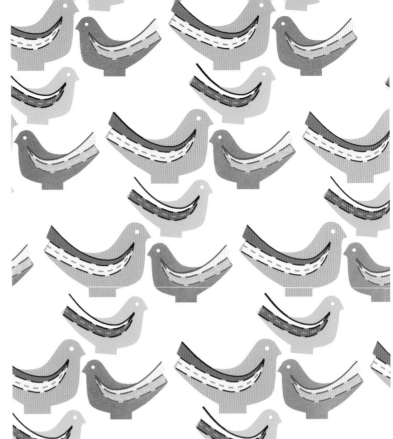

illustration (above)
navajo print

date
2007

media/techniques
adobe illustrator

illustration (above right)
birds

date
2006

media/techniques
adobe illustrator

illustration (right)
western stripe

date
2007

media/techniques
adobe illustrator

illustration (left)
floral picnic

date
2007

media/techniques
adobe illustrator

illustration (below left)
sailing away

date
2007

media/techniques
adobe photoshop

illustration (below)
floral checks

date
2007

media/techniques
adobe illustrator

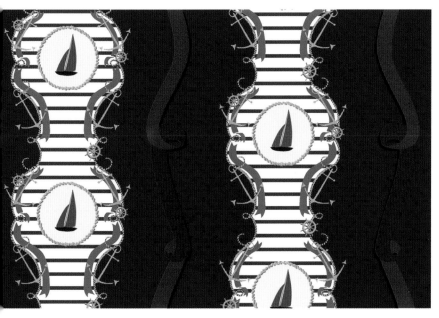

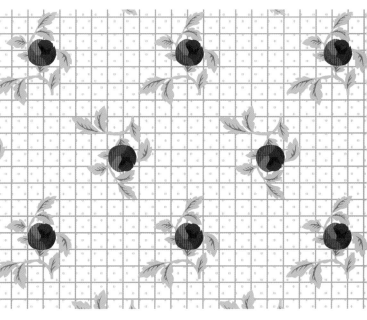

Amanda Le Donne

I grew up in Wheaton, Illinois. I realized in high school that I wanted to be a designer because all that mattered to me was how different and eccentric I looked compared to everyone around me in the conservative town in which I lived. I thought I wanted to be a fashion designer, but after enrolling in the University of Wisconsin-Madison and taking Apparel Design classes, I realized my real passion was for prints. I could be more artistic, work with colour and fully express myself better. After three years at UW-Madison, I transferred to the Fashion Institute of Technology in New York City where I spent my last year studying textile/surface design. I got my degree with a job to match and this is where I stayed. The US fashion capital has a strong grip on me now.

As a designer, I would say that I'm mostly influenced by fashion and music. I love watching the shows during fashion week on Style.com. I am most inspired by Martin Margiela. I believe he is one of the most innovative designers of my time. For a designer that uses more prints, however, there is no one that compares to Etro. Not only does she produce beautiful prints, but her sense of colour is something I will always strive to have. Music has greatly influenced my life as well and I am constantly looking for new bands to inspire me through my work. (I am currently obsessed with Arcade Fire.) If I hear a song that I love, motivation triggers inside and the creative juices flow much more easily.

When I am beginning to design a print, I always have to think about the customer. From how many colours they can afford to the sophistication and complexity of the actual artwork - this is usually the most challenging part. Usually I start by sketching ideas on paper, whether quick, crazy amounts of ideas, or focusing on drawing a certain object in very great detail, depending on the type of design. I am able to work straight from Adobe Photoshop or Illustrator also.

I currently freelance for a textile studio (The Style Council), which is a great way to do original designs. As a studio, we participate in numerous shows throughout the year in New York and Paris. There is definitely a very promising future for printed textiles. The digital age is here and the intensely complicated and amazing patterns that can now be printed digitally is astounding.

illustration
bloodshot peacock

date
2007

media/techniques
adobe photoshop

Print design is a terrific field to be in, already filled with so many talented artists. It is very easy to get lost in the shuffle in this industry, but my advice to anyone considering a career in print design is this: do not sacrifice your personal style. That is the only way to ever distinguish yourself from the ever-growing population of talented print designers. It will also help you continue to love what you spend your life doing. And that's ultimately the most important thing.

illustration (below)
mesh it up

date
2007

media/techniques
adobe photoshop

illustration (right)
coneflower

date
2005

media/techniques
gouache on water colour
paper

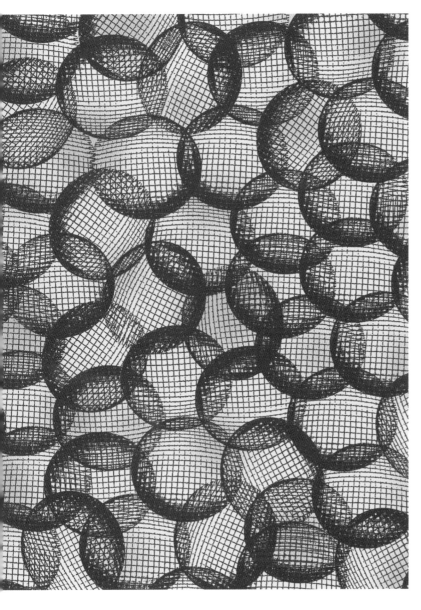

82

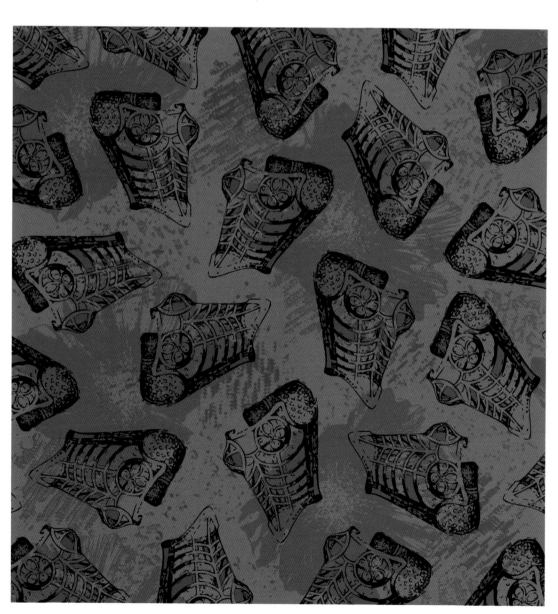

illustration (top left)
follow the blackbird

date
2007

media/techniques
adobe photoshop

illustration (top right)
purple brick house

date
2007

media/techniques
adobe photoshop

illustration (left)
armor corset engine

date
2007

media/techniques
adobe photoshop/adobe
illustrator

Lauren Engler

Although I was born in Minnesota, USA, I later moved to Palm Springs, California where I fell in love with the bright colours, 1960s architecture, palm trees and overall kitsch of the city that would later influence my work. After high school I moved to New York to attend Parsons School of Design, where I currently work and live.

I find that my work blends the quirky influences of Palm Springs with the sophisticated aesthetic of New York. The way I come across my inspiration is unpredictable, I can find inspiration in just about everything. When working on prints I always start with a sketch. A lot of my work comes from little doodles that I am constantly drawing all over my notes and sketchbooks. The layout of the print is done on the computer using both Adobe Illustrator and Photoshop. It goes from doodle to print by toying with the proportion, bringing in other sketches and playing with the rotation. I try not to restrict myself with what the print will be used for. Sometimes I think something will be great for a dress, and then I make it and want to use it as a home textile instead. I don't think much about trends; I just make whatever feels right to me. Textile design for me is an art. I like to think that a great textile would also make a great painting. Textile design incorporates all the same aspects as painting: composition, scale, colour, and subject matter.

The two most influential textiles designers for me are Eley Kishimoto and Marimekko. I think both of these labels constantly create interesting, innovative, and creative textiles. They invent textiles that work for multiple purposes from clothes, to home interiors, to products. I think it is interesting when one textile can be used in various ways.

The future of textile design will be in technology. As technology becomes more advanced there will be more and more options for printing, finishing techniques, and fabrics.

illustration
primary blocks

date
2005

media/techniques
adobe illustrator

To others who want to pursue textile design I would you say you don't need to have formal training in textile design. My background is in garment construction and fashion design. I've never taken a class in textiles but I just started sketching and creating prints that I personally liked.

Sometimes knowing nothing is the best approach.

84

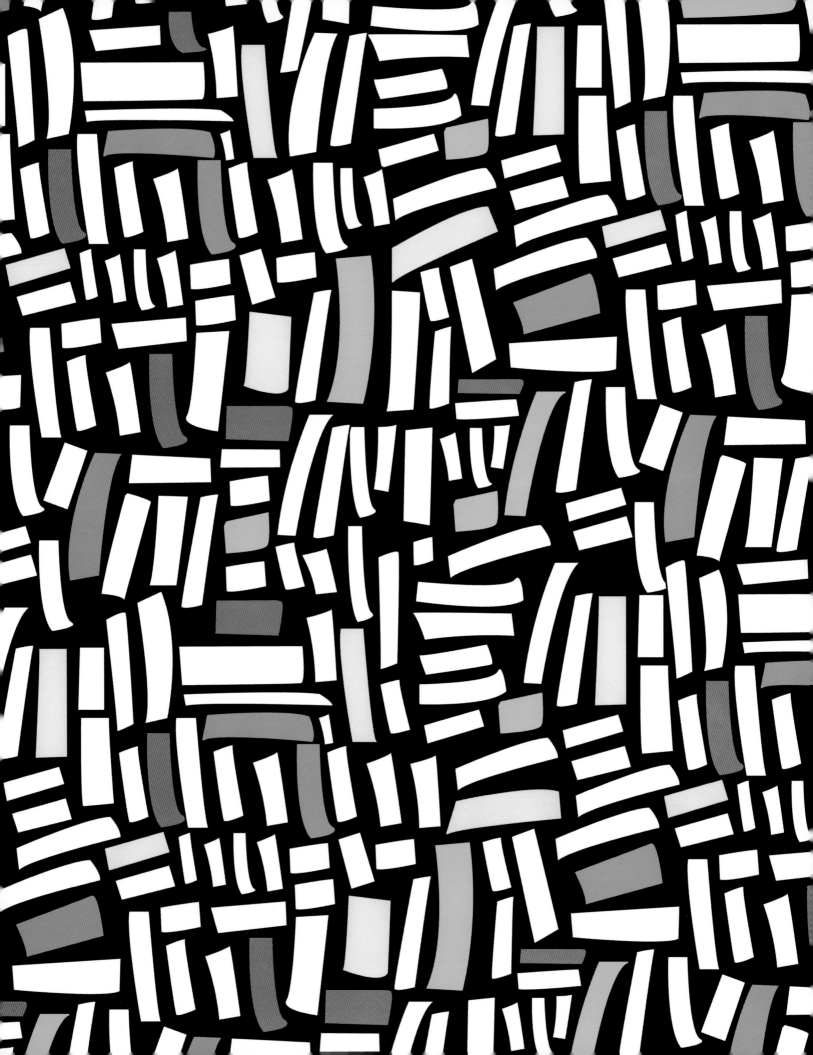

illustration (right)
modern vintage floral

date
2006

media/techniques
adobe illustrator

illustration (below)
new baroque

date
2007

media/techniques
adobe illustrator

illustration (right)
black roses

date
2006

media/techniques
adobe illustrator

illustration (right)
tropical swan

date
2007

media/techniques
adobe illustrator

illustration (below)
pop art floral

date
2006

media/techniques
adobe Illustrator

Catalina Estrada

I was born in Medellin, Colombia in 1974 where I had a lot of close contact with nature. I was raised in a house full of beautiful and particular things. My mother is an artist and she loves decorating her home and collecting beautiful objects. She has an amazing and very personal sense of beauty and has a sense of combining colours like no one else I know. Her house is painted in vivid colours. Every time I see her creations I am inspired to go to work and also use those colours in my own designs. I have always loved both art and the graphics of packaging, stickers and labels and I collect stationery. My grandmother used to collect postage stamps from all over the world and I was fascinated by these albums.

Graduating from the Universidad Pontificia Bolivariana (Medellin) with an honours degree in Graphic Design, I later travelled to Spain to study Fine Arts at Escola de Artes Llotja in Barcelona, specialising in lithography.

I now live in Barcelona where I share a studio with my husband. I enjoy working from home and have two big tables, one for my computer and one for my hand-made art. I love both digital and manual methods. When I work digitally I use Adobe Illustrator and Photoshop software. When I work by hand I love coloured pencils and watercolour on both paper and wood.

I have been very lucky to travel a lot and this has been a great influence in all I do. I take inspiration for my designs from all types of music, art – especially folk art – design, movies, and books. I particularly like Latin American artists, writers and musicians as well as both the Arts & Crafts and Art Nouveau artists with their obsession for detail. Almost anything or anyone that touches my emotions can easily inspire me. Nature has always been one of my main sources of stimulation. Barcelona has brought me into contact with lots of different cultures, it is a vibrant city that has been amazing for my work.

I usually start by sketching directly into the computer. I create my textile designs digitally because there is always the need to adjust colours, composition and size. I consider the colour balance and composition vital to my designs. Most of my designs are sold through my agent since I do not have time to visit the various trade fairs myself.

I never feel restricted by the end use of my design. The work should always flow in a natural way from inside of you. I like to see my designs translated onto different media, and it is magical when they then become someone's clothing — they come alive. Printed textiles is a field that I love working in and I hope it will continue to grow and give me many more chances of working in it.

illustration
fox pattern (paul smith)

date
2007

media/techniques
adobe illustrator

illustration (above left)

birds pattern (paul smith)

date

2007

media/techniques

adobe illustrator

illustration (left)

blue flowers (anuciacao)

date

2007

media/techniques

adobe illustrator

illustration (above)

forest (anuciacao)

date

2007

media/techniques

adobe illustrator

illustration (above)
ducks pattern (paul smith)

date
2007

media/techniques
adobe illustrator

illustration (left)
yellow flowers (anuciacao)

illustration (next page)
paloma (anuciacao)

date
2007

date
2007

media/techniques
adobe illustrator

media/techniques
adobe illustrator

91

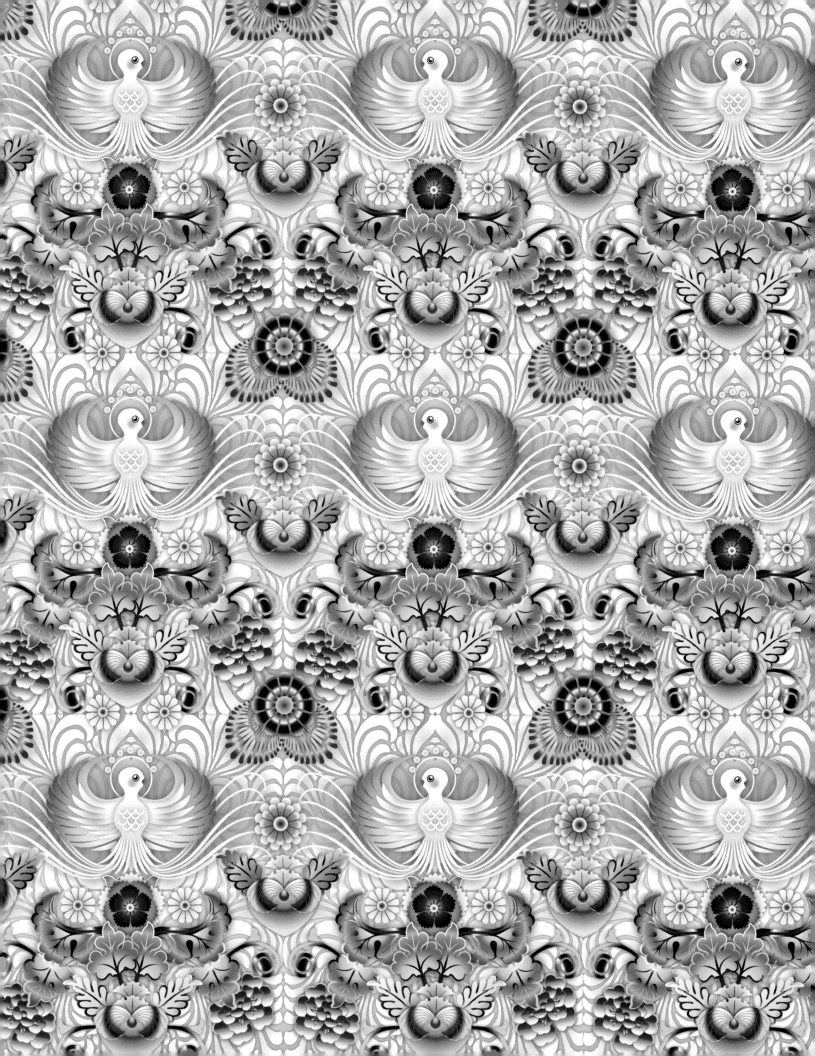

Karen Gentile

I grew up in Philadelphia and had a strong impulse for making art from a young age. I loved to draw and paint and work with clay. I was always fascinated by the idea of creating something.

I was influenced by my father who was a true Renaissance man. He built the house I grew up in and decorated the interior in black and white geometrics and abstract patterned wallpaper and fabrics. He painted murals in every room and even made the lamps and furniture, though to him it was just a hobby.

After high school I went to the Pennsylvania Academy of Fine Arts and Philadelphia College of Art for a short while. At the time, I was reading about the lives of artists in Europe and I was thunderstruck by the desire to see great art in places like Paris and Italy and embarked on a grand tour.

After many trips, I found my way to New York City and it has been my home ever since. I earned a degree at FIT in Textile/Surface Design, Restoration and Jewellery making, all the while continuing to paint and find myself as a fine artist.

I live and work in a loft in the Chelsea area of Manhattan with my husband, Richard Pitts, who is a great artist and an important influence and source of inspiration for me. I have maintained a very compatible dual career in fine art painting and working as a Textile/Surface designer and I am still passionate about both. I am a faculty member of the Textile/Surface Design department at FIT in NY and the chairperson of the department for the last four years. I teach traditional painting and print design classes as well as computer-assisted design programs such as Photoshop and Illustrator.

illustration
cubist greyscale

For Surface Design I love to paint with traditional gouache and dyes on paper and also to experiment with techniques and media of all kinds. Textile/Surface Design is a very creative field. Rich in history and an important part of culture. The exploration and discovery of techniques used in fabric creation and print and pattern used around the world is fascinating. My travel experiences in North Africa, where I personally saw these cultural art forms in the making, had a great influence on me. I also visited Greece and was captivated by the ancient Greek arts, where the fusion of art and craft is fully realized.

date
2005

media/techniques
screenprint/adobe
photoshop

I love working in all mediums but some specialties in my work are direct painting with dyes and wax resist work on silk; block printing (I have hand-cut a large number of small scale original blocks for printing on fabric and paper); screen printing and computer-assisted design – sometimes combining all of these in the creation of new designs.

94

illustration (above)
cut paper geometric

date
2005

media/techniques
paper collage/adobe
photoshop

illustration (above right)
doublet

date
2002

media/techniques
hand blockprint/adobe
photoshop

illustration (right)
prism blend

date
2003

media/techniques
adobe photoshop

illustration (left)
handpainted floral

date
2002

media/techniques
handpainted dyes on silk

illustration (far left)
crosshatch

date
1998

media/techniques
watercolour/adobe photoshop

illustration (left)
fun floral

date
2003

media/techniques
adobe photoshop

illustration (above)
handpainted silk

date
2000

media/techniques
handpainted dyes on silk

illustration (right)
floating shells

date
2003

media/techniques
scanned drawing/adobe
photoshop

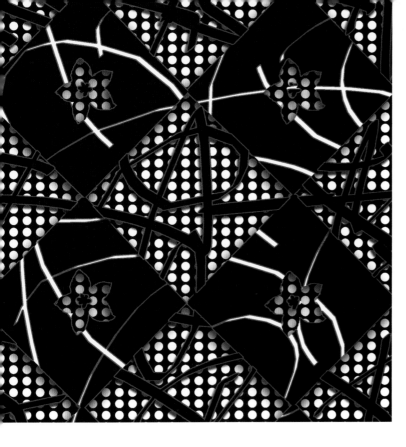

illustration (left)
calligraphic pattern

date
2005

media/techniques
adobe photoshop

illustration (below)
broken circles

date
1999

media/techniques
adobe photoshop

Jessica Michelle Nadler

From the time that I could talk I said I would be an artist. My family was nervous about this childhood dream as I did not actually make anything until around the time I turned twelve. I started obsessively drawing portraits from pictures and magazine photos and then began to develop a portfolio for college. I went on to attend the University of Michigan School of Art and Design and graduated with a dual concentration in fiber arts and printmaking. Several years later, while living in New York, I graduated with a second degree in textile and surface design from the Fashion Institute of Technology in an effort to gear my fine arts education toward the textile industry.

Age-old processes such as weaving and printmaking helped me to discover how important it is for me to be physically involved with my tools and materials. I find these methods to be challenging, stimulating and engaging – in entirely different ways than any other medium.

I gravitate toward textures, patterns and colors and find inspiration in things that I collect, nature, travel, worldwide textile and craft traditions, playing with lots of materials and from maps and photos.

Experimenting with a variety of materials and techniques can produce so many ideas that at times I am not sure which direction to follow first. This a great but overwhelming feeling. I feel most productive when I start hands-on with materials, then moving to the computer. The computer leads me to new and visually unexpected places.

It is about becoming more critical and not being afraid to completely change what I have made. This no-fear mentality helps me pave way for new ideas and designs. I think it is important to honour a design, but not to get stuck; continue to critique, revise and hopefully, improve. Although popular ideas and trends are important in any business, I find creative intuition imperative.

illustration
asian flower garden

Making art that I hope will personally impact everyday people in their everyday lives motivates me. How we style our environment and our bodies makes a creative statement about who we are and what makes us feel good. Designing pattern and textures for products that people use instead of art for art's sake makes me feel good.

date
2007

media/techniques
adobe illustrator

As we know, designs can be functional, decorative and/or a platform from which to communicate ideas and opinions. I consider textiles of all kinds an art and a craft and believe that they deserve recognition in both arenas. They are also very personal. Truly an art for life.

illustration (below)
scales

date
2007

media/techniques
adobe illustrator

illustration (below)
sunflowers

date
2007

media/techniques
adobe illustrator

illustration (left)
tulips

date
2007

media/techniques
adobe illustrator

illustration (below)
wavy lines

date
2007

media/techniques
adobe illustrator

Davina Nathan

I was born in Toronto, Canada and graduated with a BA in Art History from the University of Toronto, followed by an AAS Degree in Textile/Surface Design from the Fashion Institute of Technology in New York City.

For several years, I lived and worked in New York as a Textile Designer for the fashion and home furnishings industry. I have now returned to Toronto, to establish my own studio 'Davina Nathan Design'.

My interests since childhood have been centered on designing and creating. I was always dressing up in costumes or painting the walls with lipstick. At an early age, my mother exposed me to European collections, which resulted in an early appreciation for fine fabrics, textures and designs.

Having a passion for painting canvases and an interest in fashion, I found myself drawn to textile design, which I feel serves as a happy medium. The beauty of printed textiles is that it repeats, giving the eye a constant source of visual activity. In fashion, it is the fabric that can make or break the outfit, the printed design that captures attention in a single glance.

Textile design is an artform with limitless resources to draw upon. We are constantly influenced by everyday life, absorbing the impressions around us. There are patterns found everywhere, to be kept in a visual library in the imagination. Botanical gardens, antique fairs, folk art and the bizarre are of particular interest to me.

Strong influences belong to past eras. I especially relate to the French designers of the 40s and 50s for their linework and detail and to the ethnic designs of India, China and Japan. Some of my personal favourite designers include Arlette Chacok, Elsa Schiapparelli, Erte and Paul Poiret. Present-day design houses that appeal to me are Moschino, Etro, Paul Smith and Kenzo.

illustration
postcards from paris

When designing a print, my main considerations are simply what will make it unique, beautiful, fun (often whimsical) and make someone smile.

date
2007

It is important to be 'au courrant' — attending trade shows, reviewing trend forecasts and other inspirations resources keeping in mind you are a Designer, not a photocopier! Challenge previous conventions and find new ways to elaborate in you work.

media/techniques
watercolour and india ink on paper

Remember, a good design never falls out of fashion.

104

illustration (below)
loungecats 2

illustration (below right)
carriage ride

illustration (right)
birdcage

date
2007

date
2007

date
2006

media/techniques
watercolour and india ink on
paper

media/techniques
watercolour and india ink on
paper

media/techniques
watercolour and india ink on
paper

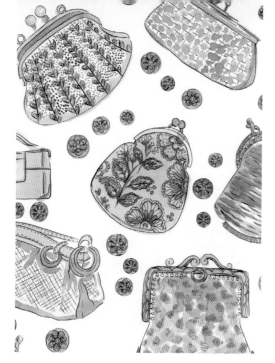

illustration (left)
vintage purses

date
2006

media/techniques
watercolour and india ink on paper

illustration (below left)
cityscape

date
2007

media/techniques
watercolour and india ink on paper

illustration (below)
flea market

date
2006

media/techniques
watercolour and india ink on paper

Open Face Sandwich designed by Laura Hoyer

Open Face Sandwich originated in 2005 with the desire to create patterns that I truly loved, that were not a result of trends and that would stand the test of time. It is a well-edited collection created by myself, along with the help of a few talented friends.

Much of my inspiration comes from being in the garden, hiking, or lazing about on the beach; in other words, nature. I grew up near the ocean in New Jersey, plus had the added benefit of having plant-, flower-, garden-, and animal-loving parents. I didn't realize what an inspiration all of this was until I was in college and continually found myself drawn to these motifs.

Although I considered majoring in fine art, I decided to study fabric at the Fashion Institute of Technology in New York City because of my interest in fashion and a desire to have a full-time job after graduation. Textile design was a perfect combination! It wasn't just the design work that I loved; I found that I also enjoyed working within the parameters that are necessary when thinking of the final printed product.

It's not just nature that inspires me. At heart, I am a city girl and that is the source of many of the geometric prints. They stem from more of an urban inspiration, such as architecture and wrought iron, as well as antique furniture and pottery seen on many museum visits. Many of the colour combinations are derived from paintings, antique swatches, posters, fashion, and interiors. This dichotomy between city and country is even present in where I work. I have studio space in Connecticut as well as in Manhattan.

Most of the designs begin as sketches or elements painted in gouache and are recreated and improved upon in Illustrator, then printed on paper. I concentrate on womens- and childrenswear, along with home and paper, because these allow for more variety and are suited to my personal style. When designing for kids in particular, I can really interject personality, quirkiness, humour, and my

illustration
ulrich

obsession for all things cute. I truly love how a pattern can evolve from something as simple as a doodle into a full color, repeated piece.

date
2007

As a new studio, I have found trade fairs to be essential. They are a great way to display your particular aesthetic and to meet new customers where they can view the entire collection. Right now is a great time to be a printed textile

media/techniques
adobe illustrator

designer! It's not just limited to fashion; patterns are everywhere and people are really embracing them.

108

illustration (above)
rosanna

date
2006

media/techniques
adobe illustrator

illustration (above)
rayen

date
2007

media/techniques
adobe illustrator

illustration (left)
blossom

date
2007

media/techniques
adobe illustrator

illustration (above)
paul

date
2006

media/techniques
adobe illustrator

illustration (above)
nydia

date
2007

media/techniques
adobe illustrator

illustration (above centre)
sergius

date
2007

media/techniques
adobe illustrator

illustration (left)
methuselah

date
2006

media/techniques
adobe illustrator

111

Janis Salek

As a textile designer, fashion illustrator and painter, almost all of my inspiration and imagery comes from the world of fashion. This world of style and image and the process of changing colors and shapes and environment; moving from season to season; couture, ready-to-wear, home, the trends, the excitement of the designers, the runway. This is the world I love and into which I pour my whole artistic life.

The way I approach textiles is to start with an idea, an inspiration for a series or group. Then I gather images, things I see or find that interest me and paint them, usually in gouache. This goes on for days or weeks until I have piles of paintings and ideas that will form the basis for my shapes. Then I trace my own work, abstract it, and generate several croquis of flat patterns. Next I research the trend resources for the colours and styles I will use and then play with them within the designs until everything comes together the way I want it. I've come to love designing on the computer in Photoshop and especially Illustrator because it's all about flat shapes and has such a contemporary look and feel.

I have drawn and painted for as long as I can remember and have always loved and been attracted to flat patterns; my mother's sofa, covered with large flowers; a puzzle map my father gave me; a large Italian floral screen gifted to my mother by an opera singer. After high school, I studied painting at the School of Visual Arts in New York and then went on to get an MFA in painting at the University of Pennsylvania. That masters program, where I could spend all my time painting, was like a dream come true.

After graduate school I returned to New York to study textile design and fashion illustration at the Fashion Institute of Technology. Also during this time, and for many years after, I studied at night with Jack Potter, the renowned fashion illustrator and teacher, who taught me to think and draw and interpret through the wonderful world of shapes. I feel so fortunate to have had that opportunity and will always be grateful for his teaching.

illustration
snow leapard floral

date
2007

media/techniques
adobe photoshop

Since then I have worked in the textile, fashion, and home furnishing industries designing womenswear, childrenswear, scarves, bedding and, most recently, wallpaper and contemporary wall coverings. I presently work as a freelance artist and designer in New York City and teach drawing and painting at the Fashion Institute of Technology, Katherine Gibbs School of Fashion, and the City College of New York. And, of course, I continue to draw and paint on a steady basis because I truly believe that working from life, filling my life with art and always trying to grow within it, is the best possible way to live.

illustration (above)

butterfly garden

date

2007

media/techniques

adobe illustrator

illustration (above right)

early spring floral

date

2006

media/techniques

adobe photoshop

illustration (right)

stripes and kimono flowers

date

2007

media/techniques

adobe illustrator

114

illustration (above left)

galaxy

date

2007

media/techniques

adobe illustrator

illustration (above)

wind blossoms

date

2007

media/techniques

adobe illustrator

illustration (left)

fairy flowers

date

2007

media/techniques

adobe illustrator

115

illustration (above)
ocean stars

date
2007

media/techniques
adobe illustrator

illustration (above right)
moon tide

date
2007

media/techniques
adobe illustrator

illustration (right)
paris fancy

date
2007

media/techniques
adobe photoshop

illustration (opposite page)
sea world

date
2007

media/techniques
adobe photoshop

Remy Steiner

I was born in Vienna, Austria. although I have lived most of my life in Northern California. I grew up in Palo Alto, and went to college in Santa Cruz and later lived in San Francisco. I am currently living and working as a freelance Print/Textile designer in Brooklyn, New York where I arrange design meetings with clients to deliver high quality design services and solutions.

During my undergraduate time in fine art at the University of California at Santa Cruz, I was lucky enough to study on a one-year printmaking course at London's Chelsea College of Art and Design. Located right in the heart of the King's Road, a mecca of fashionable boutiques.

It was while living in San Francisco that I was inspired by expert Swedish designer, Lotta Jansdotter, who had a screen-printing studio. Motivated by the idea of making things people could use, I learned how to knit, sew and crochet. I also began freelancing as a graphic designer encouraging my clients to use soy-ink dyes and recycled paper.

I applied to the Fashion Institute of Technology in New York for their AAS in Textile/Surface Design. The one-year program is the most competitive. When I received my degree, I was stunned at how much work I had produced. During my time working as a designer for Accenture, LLC, I was able travel throughout the US directing video shoots.

Because I love what I do, my hobbies are intertwined with my career: I'm always reading design and fashion magazines, taking photographs on the streets of New York and going to museums and galleries. Above all I want to make things that people will want to own and love.

I usually start my designs with a big (and quite unwieldy) idea and start sketching and deciding what materials to use. I love to paint and draw, but due to time constraints I use Illustrator and Photoshop to produce the final design. I am continuously learning new software packages and design techniques. I've also visited the Direction Show in NYC to investigate other designers.

illustration
sachiko

I believe that the future of textile design will be influenced by the materials that we use — green fabrics and environmental friendly methods. It's an exciting time to be a designer because what you choose to do will influence the future.

date
2006

My advice to new printed textile designers is to experiment. Sometimes it can seem like everything has been done — but it hasn't and each new designer

media/techniques
adobe photoshop

can always put their own spin on it to make it unique and personal.

118

illustration (below)
godzilla

illustration (right)
the bu

date
2007

date
2007

media/techniques
found map, gouache,
stamps, pen and ink

media/techniques
watercolour/adobe
photoshop

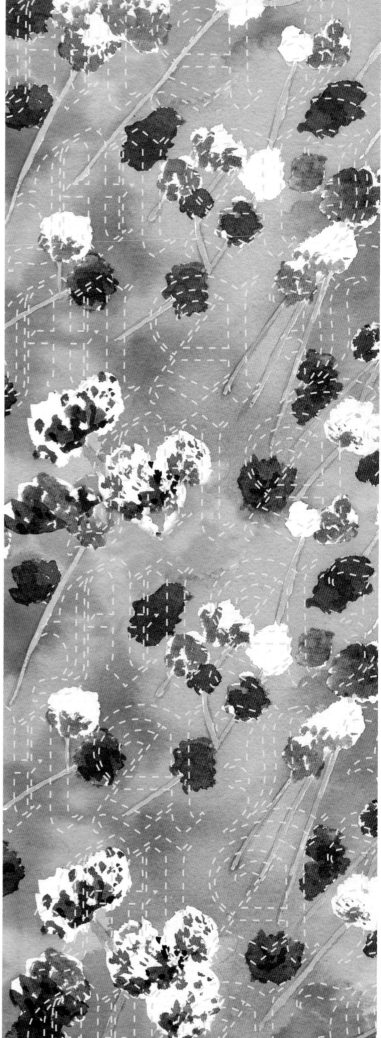

illustration (left)

topanga

date

2007

media/techniques

handpainted, adobe
photoshop

illustration (below left)

zuma

date

2007

media/techniques

gouache, pen and ink, cut
paper, found embroidered
flowers

illustration (below)

hot

date

2006

media/techniques

gouache

Jamal 'Bam' Tate

I am a fashion designer and graphic artist who started a professional career at the age of 15 as a sophomore student in New York's prestigious High School of Art & Design. As a junior, I enrolled in the City's internship program where I was drafted by the comic book publishing giant DC Comics. I attended College at the School of Visual Arts as an illustration major.

Currently, I own my own design studio 'Darkreign' working as a freelance fashion designer and graphic artist. I have a line of clothing called 'Redreign' which consist of t-shirts, leather jackets, and jewellery. I also run a workshop for those who wish to pursue a career in fashion and graphic design.

Life, nature and other artists/designers inspire me. Almost everything I see causes me to think about new ideas. One person alone cannot tell you about life, nor can one person teach you everything, or totally inspire you. So I chose to learn from everyone that crossed my path as this is an infinite pool of creativity

When I start the process of creating a textile design there are two ways it can start. One is to create the shape by hand to give the the design a more natural feel. Or I can create the shape on the computer using Adobe Illustrator. The pattern should be clean (not pixelated). Once the main object is created I may create various patterns by hand to get a feel for it or the best possible results. This process could result in ten different patterns from the original. As a professional things do change after it leaves your hands due to production constraints.

Market trends run this business — some designers will go against the grain, and I too have been known to do this. I like to create trends not really follow them.

Attending trade shows are an absolute must. I find it great to network and to see what is going on in the business.

illustration
asian velvet

date
2007

media/techniques
hand-drawing/adobe
photoshop

The future for textiles will be
-Printing from RGB
-Shapes become more basic.
-Colours more earth tone.
-Texture will come back in a major way.

From my own experiences I would pass on proper file building and professional techniques.These are the things that are not taught in colleges and universities You cannot teach creativity. Either you have it or you don't. But to be taught properly is the most important lesson of all.

122

illustration (above)
auto pattern

date
2007

media/techniques
adobe illustrator

illustration (above right)
baseball pattern

date
2007

media/techniques
adobe illustrator

illustration (right)
basketball pattern

date
2005

media/techniques
hand-drawin/adobe
illustrator

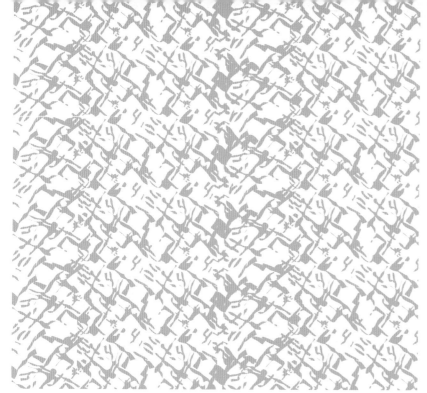

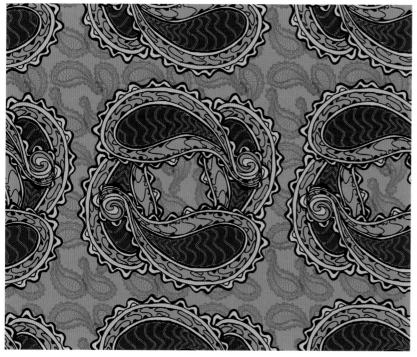

illustration (top left)	**illustration (above)**	**illustration (top right)**	**illustration (above)**
exotic skins	360-woven	paisley pouch	zebra pattern
date	**date**	**date**	**date**
2005	2004	2004	2005
media/techniques	**media/techniques**	**media/techniques**	**media/techniques**
adobe illustrator	hand-drawing/adobe illustrator	hand-drawing/adobe illustrator	adobe illustrator

125

asia

Esther Miro Bryant-Lindsay

I see textiles as the synthesis of art, craft, fashion and design, which merges these disciplines in a way that allows them to complement and aid each other into a unique and exciting design medium. My interest in textile design evolved from my interest in fashion, art and craft throughout my adolescence. I experimented with my creativity when I studied towards a Bachelor of Fine Arts at Ilam School, but it was working for Wearable Art, which inspired me to do textile design and my degree at Massey fused my passions for fashion, art and textiles.

Printed textiles has always been interesting to me because of the way the medium allows you to translate your ideas from drawings, mark-making and photography to textiles. I often choose to experiment with a range of media to create a variety of textures and I especially enjoy bringing texture to screen-printing, which is so often used for just flat colour designs.

As a designer, the influence of art, music, film, fashion and pop culture all play key roles in my work. I often find inspiration from art, high-end fashion and textiles, magazines, books and the environment around me. I am attracted to vintage clothing and the textiles applied in these. I love reinventing a past style in a contemporary aesthetic. I have a fixation with the pattern-on-pattern look and I think vintage clothing is a wonderful source for this approach. Once my design has taken its form in a fabric sample I am open-minded to the prospect of 'repeat'.

illustration
vintage garden 1

date
2005

media/techniques
sublimart on synthetic fabric

As a recent graduate I haven't gained a lot of experience with market trends. But I think in a commercial sense it is greatly important to be aware of current trends and trend prediction. This is an area that interests me and I hope to learn more about it in the near future. I see the future of printed textiles becoming a lot more radical and intricately detailed. Printed textiles have really made a come-back in the fashion industry. I think digital textiles are becoming a lot more affordable and accessible and we will continue to see the industry grow. What I hope to see in the future is textile designers working towards innovative ways to create sustainable alternatives within the textile industry.

To anyone thinking of studying textile design I say 'go for it!' If you like art, apparel, interior, print, colour and styling you'll love it. It's an amazing area to get into, which offers a wide range of skills.

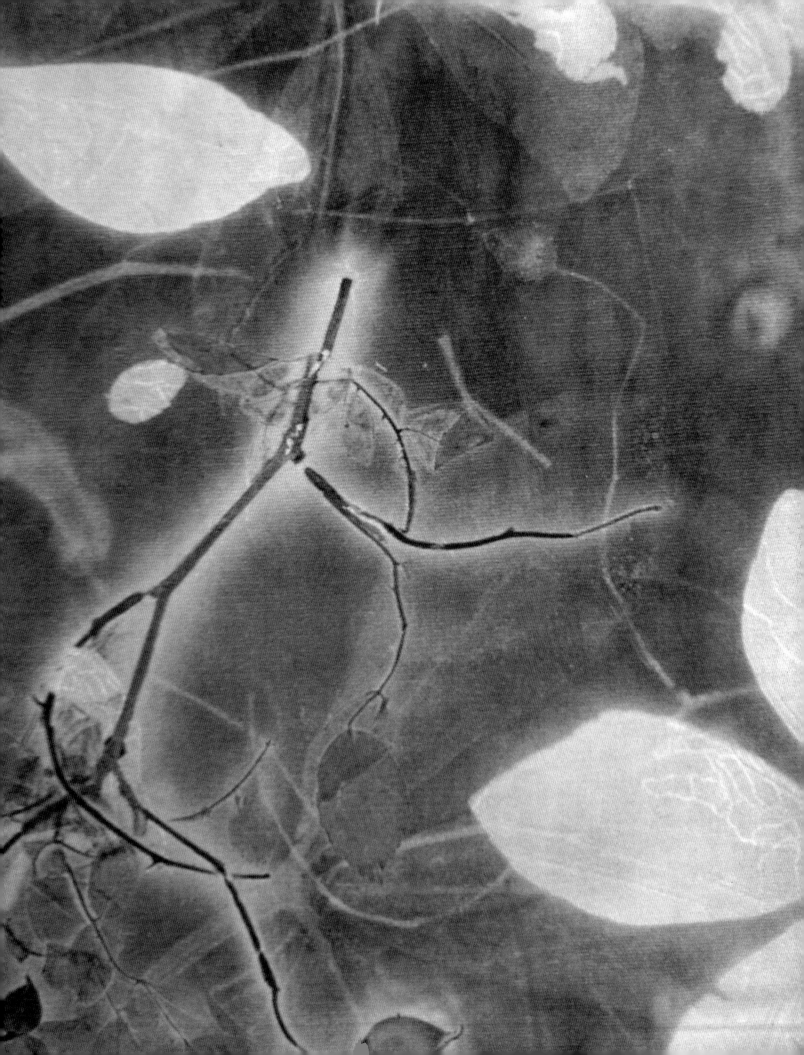

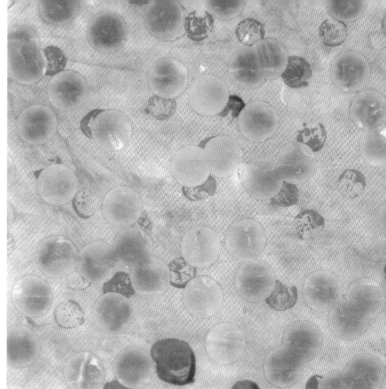

illustration (above)
vintage garden 2

date
2005

media/techniques
sublimart on synthetic fabric

illustration (above right)
vintage garden 3

date
2005

media/techniques
sublimart on synthetic fabric

illustration (right)
vintage garden 4

date
2005

media/techniques
sublimart on synthetic fabric

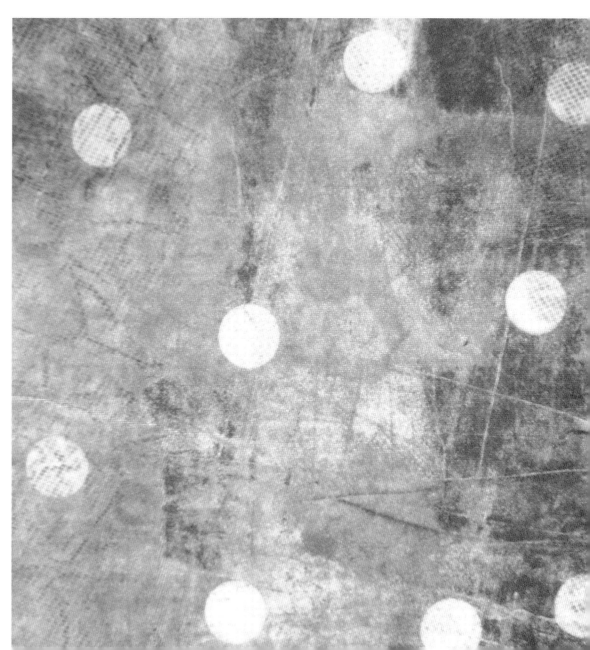

illustration (left)
vintage garden 5

illustration (above)
vintage garden 6

date
2005

date
2005

media/techniques
sublimart on synthetic fabric

media/techniques
sublimart on synthetic fabric

Georgia Chapman

For as long as I can remember, I've collected bits of cloth, decorative paper, old scarves, pieces of wallpaper – anything that appeals to me for colour and surface decoration. It seemed only natural that I became a textile designer.

For me, textile design is a fusion of fine art and design. The 'art' is about mark making, research, history, colour; the 'design' is how it is all applied.

My grandmother was a textile designer and my mother would make things with me from a young age. I was best at art-based subjects at school so I studied Art and Design in a TOP course. I went on to study at RMIT completing a BA in textile design where I learnt the tools of my trade.

My first full-time job was working for a large Australian fashion company, which I found to be soul destroying. A friend had similar feelings, so we agreed to join forces and went on to work together for 8 years under the label Vixen.

I took our first range of scarves to show David Jones and Georges and they wanted to buy them. We were offering something different to the mass-produced product. The business started growing and we did a lot of design and hand-printing for other fashion companies.

Although my business partner later left the business, I was keen to capitalise on the good relationships we were developing with retailers. I never want the business to become mass-produced and lose its essence.

It is hard to articulate the way I design a range because a lot of that evolves intuitively. I'm constantly taking in things and collecting things wherever I go but it might take a while for that idea to actually come to fruition in a range. I'm always observing and absorbing. Sometimes one range will flow naturally into the next, sometimes the creative direction will change, but always with the Vixen 'signature'.

illustration
monet 1

I have an innate sense of femininity and what females want to wear. That feminine quality is definitely from my mother – she's very womanly, nurturing and soft and there was a real naturalness about the way I was brought up. This had a big influence on me and it still affects the way I live today.

date
2005

I like to create a cohesive and recognisable 'look' – I avoid following transient trends and fads. I like the idea that people can wear pieces from one range with something they may have owned for a few years. I want them to feel that they've made a good investment.

media/techniques
handpainted acid dyes on
silk crepe de chine

illustration (above)

garden party

date

2004

media/techniques

handpainted acid dyes on
silk satin

illustration (above right)

ikat

date

1996

media/techniques

digital print on silk satin

illustration (left)	illustration (above)	illustration (above)
chinoiserie	monet 2	mikado
date	**date**	**date**
1996	2005	2005
media/techniques	**media/techniques**	**media/techniques**
handprinted bleach print on viscose jersey	handpainted acid dyes on silk crepe de chine	handpainted acid dyes on silk jacquard

Smriti Gupta

I was born in the northern Indian town of Varanasi known for its rich culture and the Holy Ganges. My early schooling was at Rishi Valley School, KFI, and it was here that I discovered my passion for art.

I take my inspiration from all aspects of nature, be it in art, photographs or drawings. For me nature has both form and abstraction. It was the late Mrs Pupul Jayaker, the pioneer of the Indian craft industry and the founder of design education in India, whose lecture at school inspired me to take this hobby forward as a profession.

With the support of my parents, I continued my studies at the National Institute of Design in Ahmedabad, where I majored in Textile Design. I now live in New Delhi where I head a design studio, Studio Smriti, working with some of the best design and fashion houses in India.

I believe that print is the most flexible and fluid medium for use in textiles. Almost any idea can be translated perfectly with the application of today's printing techniques, making it possible to replicate the original design. Indian art and crafts are the most important and dominant influence on my work.

I prefer to start a design with hand drawing and watercolours. I enjoy working in water or poster paints and then I spend hours using Adobe Photoshop to create different effects. With the flexibility of today's software I really enjoy trying different effects at the click of a mouse.

I really admire the work of Vincent van Gogh. The way he combined abstraction with the real world always fascinates me. His self portrait with a bandaged ear is among my favourites.

Although market trends are essential, a unique design is equally important. I think elements from the trends can be incorporated in any design to help cater to the wider needs of the market.

illustration
adbhut

date
2006

media/techniques
adobe photoshop

Prints already represent the most employed technique in textiles. The flexibility of the technique and the cost effectiveness makes it the most versatile of all textile techniques. Print is evolving and the concept of placement prints is taking the lead in both home and garment applications.

My advice to any student thinking of embarking on a career in textile design is to follow your heart and enjoy the work that you are doing. Only if you enjoy your work will the designs will be successful.

136

illustration (right)
jailasmer

date
2003

media/techniques
adobe photoshop

illustration (far right)
mogra

date
2002

media/techniques
adobe photoshop

illustration (right)
utsav

date
2005

media/techniques
adobe photoshop

illustration (far right)
prem

date
2006

media/techniques
adobe photoshop

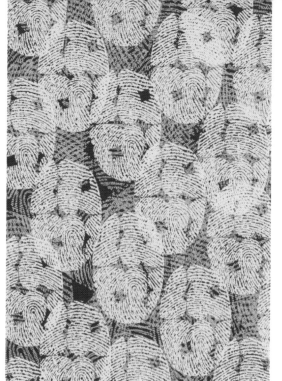

illustration (above left)
akriti

date
2005

media/techniques
adobe photoshop

illustration (above)
roshini

date
2005

media/techniques
oil paint/adobe photoshop

illustration (left)
tara

date
2005

media/techniques
oil paint/watercolour/adobe
photoshop

Hoon Ju Ko

I was born and grew up in Korea. My own artistic sensitivity comes directly from my mom who has a natural feel for art. I graduated from B.F.A and M.F.A in Seoul where I used to paint on to fabric and photography. I was always interested in discovering and investigating new ideas from the wide variety of materials that I worked with.

After I graduated, I first worked in a local fashion apparel company before moving to America. New York City has pulsating energy and is constantly exciting. I can always get inspiration from what is going on around me – out on the street, up on the wall, in the museum, even in Barnes & Noble or Starbucks. That is why I love living in New York City.

While travelling to other countries I saw many artistic fabrics, notes and wall print designs which inspired me to become a designer. I chose to be a textile designer because I love drawing and painting on to fabric surfaces.

My designs always stem from my very personal influences. I love to go out to the hardware store and get very excited when I see the wide variety of supplies such as bolts, wire, net, woods, plastic, rubber, tape and so on. My own design style has now developed its own unique manner that is not a recognised form. I always try to create new ideas out of the known – like a soft rectangle, a tough flower, a dot from a rock. In nature it might just be a pretty flower, but its geometry and pattern presents perfectly clean lines.

I admire the British artist Francis Bacon, who painted many screams in his works. He developed an excellent way of combining powerful shapes with bright colour. For the same reason I also love Frida Kahlo.

I enjoy watching art films and reading the many art and design books and fashion magazines. I allow all of these influences to stimulate fresh ideas that gain fresh expression in my own design work.

illustration
leaves

I use Adobe Photoshop and my own hand-drawn techniques. I always want to make my textile design as artistic as possible, as in a painting, so that they can be seen as important art works in their own right.

date
2007

When designing it is always important to consider market trends because they ultimately dictate the new season's trends and ideas and cannot be ignored.

media/techniques
adobe photoshop

Textile design is such a wonderful area to work in and it is within each of us to discover and relish this fantastic patterned world.

illustration (above)
animal

date
2006

media/techniques
adobe photoshop

illustration (above right)
moon reed

date
2007

media/techniques
adobe photoshop

illustration (right)
sinla crown

date
2007

media/techniques
adobe photoshop

142

illustration (left)
forest

illustration (above)
ice

date
2006

date
2007

media/techniques
hand drawn

media/techniques
adobe photoshop

Kyujin Lee

Although I was born in Seoul and grew up in Korea, I came to England to carry out my art education at Central Saint Martins in London. After graduating from their BA Fashion Women's Wear course I stayed on and eventually graduated from their MA Design for Textiles Futures.

I am currently employed as a Professor in the Department of Fibre and Fashion at Mokwon University back home in Korea where I also indulge in my own work as a practising freelance designer/artist. I view my own designs as both art- and craft-based expressions. My work is about the possibility of creating a visual narrative through textiles and fashion.

When I was growing up in Korea I always liked drawing from my imagination. I liked to make up stories. Today, I like to print my stories onto fabric – I treat it like a visual narrative on cloth. It is always important for me to develop my own stories through my work.

I take inspiration from the personal environment that I encounter. I am really interested in the domestic setting which has prompted me to identify my designs along the lines of a 'Domestic Theatre'.

I take my imagery from distressed walls, broken hangers, discarded hats and used T-shirts – all to establish the main 'characters'. The markings and traces left on them by time are the key elements that then help to establish the narratives. These found objects are documented by photography and manipulated digitally, mixed with hand-drawings, attempting to produce patterns that would suit textile prints.

I like to imagine something new from old and used items and transform them into something unexpected and fresh. I let the design develop naturally. Once created, the image is then digitally printed onto fabric.

illustration
hanger pattern

I really like the work of Sarah Sze, Hella Jongerius, Bless, the Droog Design Group, Bernhard Willhelm, Wolfgang Tillman and Walter Van Beirendonck.

date
2004

I find visiting the main trade fairs gives me incentive to create my own designs. Although it is important to consider market trends, it is equally important not to lose the originality that each design can provide.

media/techniques
adobe photoshop/digital
print

Although I remain uncertain where printed textiles is heading in the future, my personal advice to all budding textile designers is to gain as much experience as possible – it really is amazing fun when you know how to do it.

144

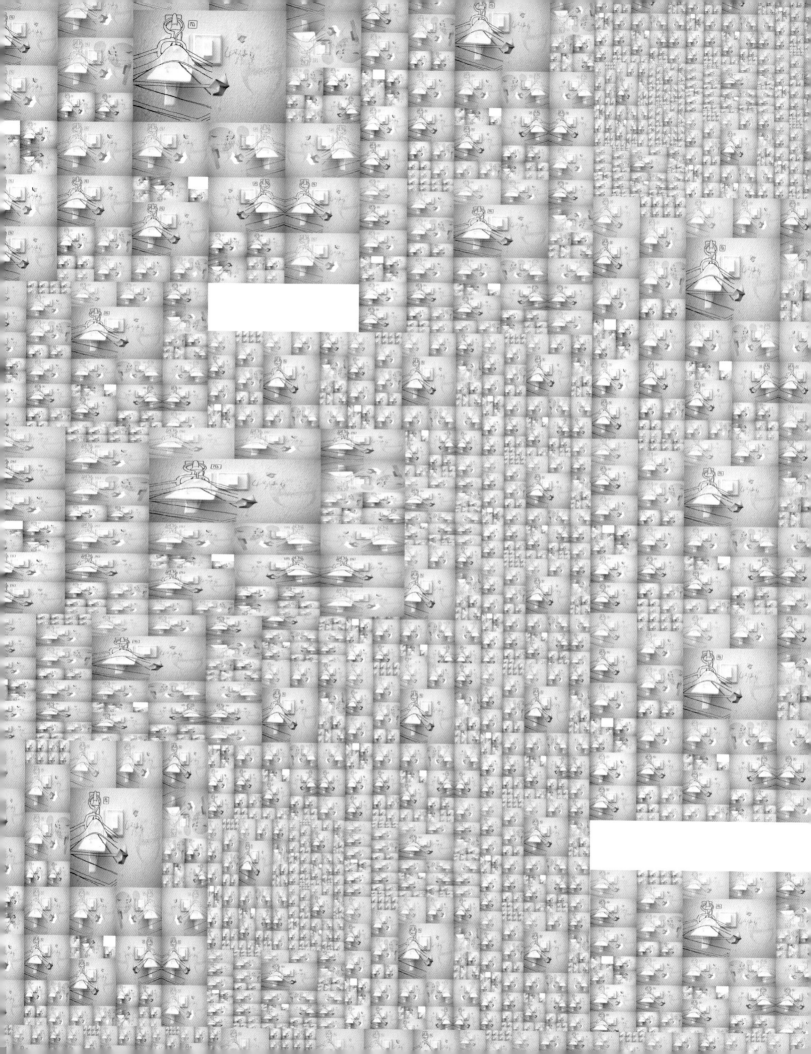

illustration (above)
bird 1

date
2004

media/techniques
adobe photoshop/digital
print

illustration (right)
hanger 3

date
2005

media/techniques
adobe photoshop/digital
print

146

illustration (far left)
ice mountain 2

date
2005

media/techniques
adobe photoshop/digital
print

illustration (left)
ice mountain 4

date
2005

media/techniques
adobe photoshop/digital
print

illustration (far left)
towel mountain 2

date
2005

media/techniques
adobe photoshop/digital
print

illustration (left)
towel mountain 5

date
2005

media/techniques
adobe photoshop/digital
print

Longina Phillips Designs

I was born in Poland and came out to Australia when I was 15 years old with my family. We knew no English and we had no possessions, so beginning a new life on the other side of the world was a very big adventure.

I currently live in Sydney and have my studio (Longina Phillips) and a team of designers based in Surry Hills, close to the city. This was traditionally a fashion area so the building we are in has a lot of character – it is a great space.

According to Mum and Dad, being a designer was not a real job. Yet after completing a three-month placement as an architect and hating it, I decided to do Graphic Design instead.

I did a four-year Visual Communications course at UTS in Sydney where I discovered the world of fabrics – I found an industry that I did not know existed, the world of pattern and colour.

I think that my heritage has a lot to do with what I find inspiring. I have lived in two different cultures – one where we had very little and one where everything is possible, so I look for things that are positive, uplifting, and happy.

I find inspiration everywhere – shopping, holidays, art gallerys, watching movies, opera, bookshops, watching people on the street. It might depend what season or theme we are working on but suddenly we find inspiration in unusual places. I like very strong graphics, uncluttered statements, and everything that is beautifully drawn.

We are a commercial studio who always consider the seasons and colour. We follow market trends and visit trade fairs – it is important to know what people are doing, to get new ideas, to meet people, to network, and also to know what not to do.

illustration
utopia

For us everything starts with a drawing, which is then scanned into the computer. We add texture, colour, pattern, photos. This gives our designs their own identity, we use computers but the designs are never computer-driven. Although we work on paper we can output digitally directly onto silk, cotton, wool and leather at the studio.

date
2007

With the availability of direct digital printing on to fabrics, the future offers so many more possibilities. Inkjet printing on to textiles offers a new aesthetic,

media/techniques
adobe photoshop

new rules or lack of rules, such as no engraving of screens, no repeats, unlimited colours – everything seems possible.

148

illustration (above)
summer

date
2004

media/techniques
adobe photoshop

illustration (above right)
kaleidoscope

date
2006

media/techniques
adobe photoshop

illustration (right)
kate

date
2005

media/techniques
adobe photoshop

illustration
midnight jungle

date
2006

media/techniques
adobe photohop

151

152

illustration
kyoto red

date
2007

media/techniques
adobe photoshop

Amy Van Luijk

Colour is my main inspiration. I live and work in New Zealand and the light here is very special. During the day we have sharp, bright, clear colours, but in the evening the palette changes with unpredictable and often amazing results. There are so many beautiful colour palettes around us. We have spectacular natural scenery with its strong and vivid greens and its calming blues. But I also love the colours of the manmade scenery in the cities. When the sun goes down at night the windows of the apartments in Wellington come to life with a glow and sparkle that is truly delicious.

Each of my designs reflects something from my environment. I constantly collect things and images that appeal to me. Inspiration can come from other visual arts, like photography, architecture or bookbinding, but also from literature. A project begins with drawings, many drawings. With pencil, paper, a photocopier and glue I go through a long and messy process of development and selection. Often in the final work my original source is no longer identifiable. The main thing is to hold on to the real reason why something attracted my attention in the first place.

I admire the Japanese art/design aesthetic: from the old Hiroshige prints to contemporary artists such as Aya Takano and Yoshitomo Nara. The simplicity of these artists' work appeals to me. They use just the right amount of colour and pattern. For the same reason, I am inspired by Haruki Murakami's writing. I love the attention to detail in his stories, and how every sentence has just enough words to describe the scene, and no more.

I aim for a similar effect in my work. The combination of attention to detail and economy of description is truly important in textile design. The final product must work at different scales and from different distances: from close-up, to arms-length, and even across a room. I have to satisfy my love of intricate detail (I still have my old stamp collection), without losing sight of the big picture. I love the challenge of designing repeat patterns. There is a real skill in making a successful repeat pattern and it is so rewarding when it works! I like to design patterns where the repeat is subtle and not immediately visible.

illustration
pretty in post

date
2006

media/techniques
mixed media /adobe photoshop

I chose to work in textile design because it is so versatile. I love that at the end of the design process you have produced something that someone can not only look at, and enjoy, but also wear and use. Some people would see that as a limitation to their freedom of expression, but for me it opens up another dimension of communication with my audience.

illustration (above left)
capturing fragments 3

date
2006

media/techniques
hand screen printed with
reactive dyes and batik

illustration (left)
splendid ruins 1

date
2007

media/techniques
paper/collage/drawing/paint

illustration (above)
eye in the sky

date
2007

media/techniques
hand screen printed

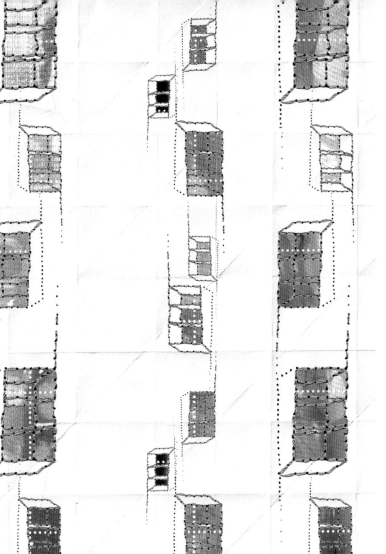

illustration (above left)

pretty in post 3

date

2006

media/techniques

mixed media/adobe
photoshop

illustration (above)

capturing fragments 1

date

2006

media/techniques

hand screen printed with
reactive dyes and batik

illustration (left)

capturing fragments 5

date

2006

media/techniques

hand drawn/adobe
photoshop

157

Saori Okabe

Although I was born in Japan and grew up in Kyoto, I went to High School in New Zealand, returning to Japan for two years to study Product Design. Further to that I had the opportunity to go over to Scotland to study Printed Textile design for three years at Edinburgh College Art. Currently, I'm living in Italy and working for a fashion company.

When I was young, my grandfather, who ran a tie company, always gave me leftovers of yarn and scrap fabric to play with and I often made pictures with them – using them like paint. At the time, I never thought that I wanted to become a designer, but I was always interested in art. It was a way to express myself without using language. It was a real turning point for me.

I think fabric is always close to peoples' lives. For me fabric has infinite possibilities to change shape and texture on contact with a surface. Even today, I like weaving fabrics into patterns and then printing onto their surface.

I do take inspiration from what I see and what I do. I believe that every second my eyes are working like scanners, recording visual reference that I translate into my designs. I believe that enjoying the quality of life around me is the single most important thing that stimulates my design creation. I would encourage all designers to absorb as much inspiration as possible just like when they were children. The main influence on my own work is always nature. I always want to my work to be totally natural.

In my design work I think 90% style and about 10% technique. I prefer to work straight off with first-hand sketches and drawings – definitely no photographs. I play with scale to see the work from different viewpoints and test out lots of possible patterns to see which looks best. I never give up on a design until I feel really comfortable with it.

illustration
drawing 6

I really like the fashion style of Missoni and Cacharel and the expression of painters like Gustav Klimt and Marc Chagall. I like their methods of mixing colour and scale, which I find very gentle to the eyes.

date
2006

It is always important to consider the business of fashion and to understand social demands. I like to visit trade fairs to keep up to date with developments although I always keep an open mind.

media/techniques
paper collage/adobe
photoshop

I do believe that there is no correct or strict way to becoming a designer. That is the great thing about being an artist, by feeling free and listening to what you feel from your heart, you will easily find your own way.

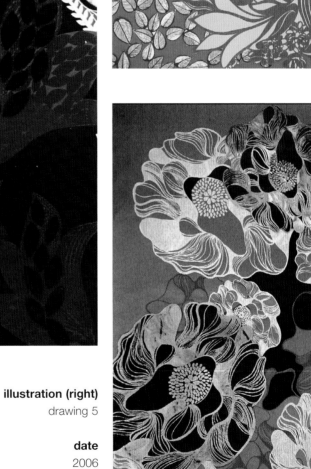

illustration (above)	illustration (above right)	illustration (right)
drawing 1	drawing 2	drawing 5
date	**date**	**date**
2006	2006	2006
media/techniques	**media/techniques**	**media/techniques**
paper collage/adobe photoshop	paper collage/adobe photoshop	paper collage/adobe photoshop

illustration (above)
drawing 3

date
2006

media/techniques
paper collage/adobe
photoshop

illustration (above)
drawing 4

date
2006

media/techniques
paper collage/adobe
photoshop

Faizal Reza

I grew up in Kuala Lumpur, Malaysia and studied Graphic Design in college. I still live and work in Kuala Lumpur, Malaysia. I love my country!

I always knew that I would be a designer, even when I was still in primary school. Initially I studied mechanical engineering, but was quite bad at it except for 'mechanical drawing', so I knew then that Art & Design was something for me. I'm more interested in creating something visual on paper as opposed to burying my head in a book full of words.

I always consider my designs as art because I do not craft it directly onto the fabric surface. I'm inspired by street art. I made a trip to Europe and saw some great street art in Barcelona. That was really inspiring.

I also take inspiration from my family. Here is a story of how I came to develop my personal style of patterning. I've always been a computer guy, where I naturally created things with the computer. One day I was with my daughter when she was just 11 months old and I had a piece of paper and started doodling on it. The doodle turned out to be quite interesting and the result is the style you now see in my work.

It is 'good design' that turns me on as a designer. It can come in any form, be it art, billboard, posters, websites, furniture, music videos, music and even the odd CD cover. The lines are so blurred nowadays because you can see art in any medium.

I work with pencil, marker pen, paper and the computer. I always start to sketch/draw the initial main patterns with a pencil and paper and then I scan them into the computer to layout and play with the colours. I sometimes find that the colours that I see on the screen don't always translate as vibrantly when printed. I'm still in the process of getting used to that.

illustration
gula-gula

date
2007

media/techniques
hand-drawn /adobe
illustrator

Fashion design and trends generally operate in a circular cycle. Something that you consider old now might well come back in the future as something really cool. It will always evolve with extra ideas to fit with the times.

I always believe if you have a particular style that people love, then you should stick to it and evolve it. Become a trendsetter rather than a follower. Always be original and try to find from within you a personal style.

illustration (previous page)

aresha

illustration (above)

fphuew

date

2006

date

2007

media/techniques

hand drawn/adobe illustrator

media/techniques

hand drawn/adobe illustrator

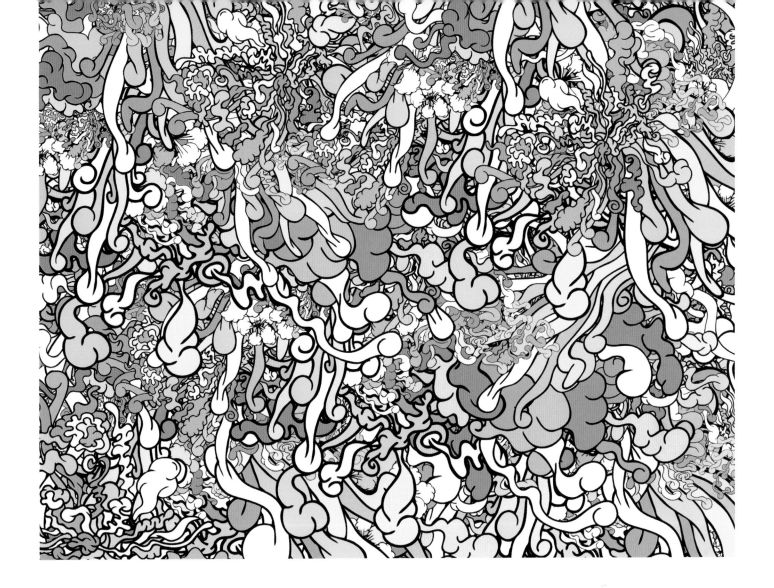

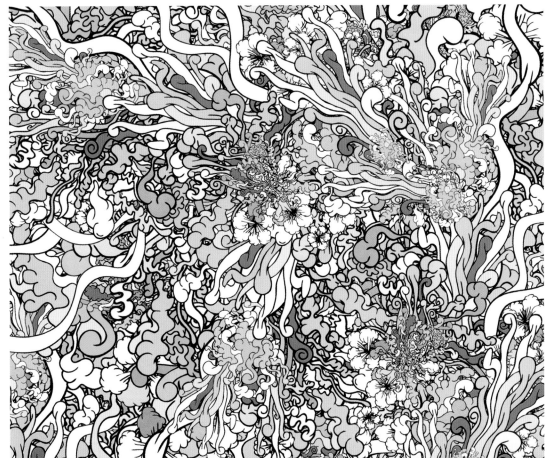

illustration (above)
fall

date
2007

media/techniques
hand drawn/adobe illustrator

illustration (left)
shiver

date
2007

media/techniques
hand drawn/adobe illustrator

Stewart Russell

Born in Scotland, I studied Fine Art both in England and Canada. Since then an art practice, curating contemporary art exhibitions and printing onto fabric have been the three constants on a creative journey that has seen me set up studios in Sri Lanka, Edinburgh, Colombia, London and, since January 2000, Melbourne, Australia.

My art projects start with a fixation on a subject and develop, like a hobby, through the informal gathering of information and obsessive collecting of ephemera. These projects, often looking at heritage and our collective cultural inheritances, are characterised by an engaging and accessible subject, homespun and disrupted classification methodologies and ambitious production values. The projects are often unconventional, usually politically engaged, and consistently concerned with how the ideas presented exist and how they might be disseminated.

My ideas for design projects are often driven by my fascination with traditional textile design and new directions in contemporary art. The studio still has strong ties with London and Tokyo but the influences and design themes developed for art projects and design collections are generated from living and working in Melbourne. Exhibition projects and fashion deadlines create intense periods where new design work emerges by necessity. But outside these key periods of design activity my studio makes time every day to work on new print ideas and printing techniques. Some ideas are slow burning and take months or even years to develop through to production, others are resolved within a few hours of coming up with the concept.

Above all I am adaptable – the design and printing processes aren't fixed and anything can happen, be changed or modified. Even the printing machinery and equipment comes and goes.

Another ongoing influence is the studio backing cloth that covers the sample print table. The table is used solely for experimentation and print development and becomes saturated with print ideas and colour tests. The cloth is replaced every 8 weeks or so and amongst the build up of printed ideas I often find chance compositions. I am at pains to keep my art and design work distinctly separate, therefore the backing cloth is the only time the two areas of creative practice truly come together. The studio has a waiting list for backing cloth pieces, now prized by collectors, as a chaotic historical record of my creative output and my collaborative projects. Although essentially a byproduct of the creative process they, perhaps more than any single piece of design or artwork, manage to capture the energy of my studio in full flight.

illustration
untitled

date
2007

media/techniques
screenprint

illustration
untitled

date
2007

media/techniques
screenprint

illustration (above)
untitled

illustration (next page)
untitled

date
2007

date
2007

media/techniques
screenprint

media/techniques
screenprint

Yoshiko Saito

I was born and raised in Japan. I had always wanted to study something creative so I enrolled in a Foundation Art course in Paris. During this time I made the decision to pursue studying design and discovered textile design at the Chelsea College of Art and Design. For me textile design incorporates my passion for drawing, my love of patterns and motifs, my fascination of texture and touch, and the enthusiasm I have for finding the perfect combinations of colours.

I have always been fascinated by all kinds of decorative art since I was small. From all kinds of wood carving, to decorative wrought iron work, from jewellery and wallpapers to tiles, carpets and fabrics – I can happily spend hours admiring the small details and how perfectly they are designed. I am trying to achieve this idea of flawless motif patterns in my own work.

After almost a decade of living abroad, I came back to Tokyo where I am currently living and creating my work. When it comes to inspiration, I think a lot it comes from nature, but I am also constantly being inspired by people's clothes, accessories and also by pieces of art and interior decors that I see when I am out.

I work mainly with agents located in New York and London. They attend trade fairs and keep me updated with trends and forecasts, as it is important to be aware of the market trend. I create designs that I'd actually like to wear. After considering a trend forecast as well as my own market research on people and shops in Tokyo to get an idea of the current mood, I start by making a motif by drawing it using Photoshop or cutting out papers using a design knife. I play with the motif and layout until I feel it is right.

illustration
cut square 3

I think about the colour palette by imagining different occasions and times of the day that I might wear such a fabric. When I am designing, I think about the final shape of a garment and how the pattern will appear when the fabric is on a person's body, pleated or manipulated, not just how it appears when lying on a flat surface. Then I print the design onto a fabric, and cut and sew them into a garment shape.

date
2007

media/techniques
adobe photoshop

As we see more consideration of the final product influencing our designing, I think the future role of the textile designer for fashion will merge with that of the fashion designer. Also taking into consideration the rapid development of printing technology enabling us to print a much larger variety of textile designs, I think this will allow us to meet people's various needs and trends better in the future.

illustration (above)
cut out 3

date
2007

media/techniques
adobe photoshop

illustration (above)
cut out 4

date
2007

media/techniques
adobe photoshop

illustration (above right)
overlap florals 4

date
2007

media/techniques
adobe photoshop

illustration (right)
cut florals 5

date
2007

media/techniques
adobe photoshop

illustration (above)

nikitageo

date

2007

media/techniques

adobe photoshop

illustration (top left)

ring geo

date

2007

media/techniques

adobe photoshop

illustration (above)

line and bluedia

date

2007

media/techniques

adobe photoshop

Sandra Setyawan

I chose printed textiles because it was inherited from my Indonesian family. My father deals with the ink systems in the textile industry. So ever since I was little, I have been aware of the textile industry. The rest of my family like going to shops to buy material and make them into clothes, so I visited fabric shops quite often. What I like about the medium is that there are so many different types of fabrics: the softness and thickness and how the fabrics fall on our skin. It is the application of printed textiles that I really like.

I later studied in England where I graduated from the London College of Communication with a BA in Surface Design and I now currently live and work in Bandung, Indonesia.

Although it was fashion and film that first turned me towards design things that happen around me in daily life can also provide my inspiration. I have travelled in Bali, Asia and Europe, and I always look at the traditional customs in each city I have visited. What is the weather like, how are the people, what kind of lifestyle do the locals have? I really like textured objects.

From my own experience, to become a good printed textile designer, you have to observe things that are happening around you. You can never imagine how these simple things can be the starting point to a fabulous design. I always admired the French artist, Georges Seurat.

I start my own designs when I remember countries or cities I have visited. When I travel, I always take lots of photographs to back up my research. I also use my sketch book. From the photographs, I may use photocopies to generate a lot of ideas that I never thought about before: enlarging the picture, or distorting and shrinking the photograph to see the changes. Then I work them up into textile patterns. It is always important for me to know the end use of my designs. I particularly like to design for fabrics, paper and ceramics.

illustration
kampoeng daun 1

date
2006

media/techniques
adobe photoshop

Market trends are equally important, such as the colourway or what kind of motif is considered a good design for a particular season. I visit European trade fairs such as Premier Vision and Como Crea to see what each of the different studios has produced. Sometimes the approach in studio shows is different from the work presented for the buyers.

There are certain things I always consider when designing that depend on the design I'm doing at the time. If it's a geometric pattern, then I produce it as a true repeat design. If it's a flowing repeat, normally I only indicate that it's a repeat design.

178

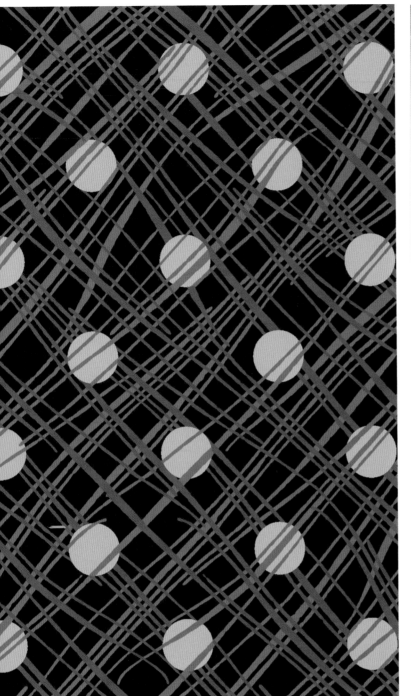

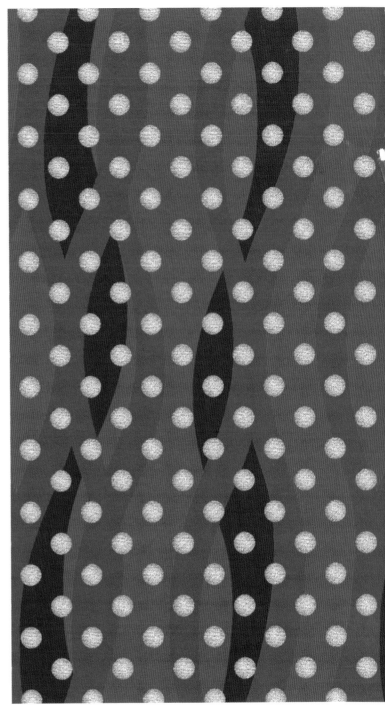

illustration (above)
colour and patterns
exploration 3

date
2006

media/techniques
adobe photoshop

illustration (above)
colour and patterns
exploration 1

date
2006

media/techniques
adobe photoshop

illustration (opposite right)
old and new

date
2006

media/techniques
adobe photoshop

180

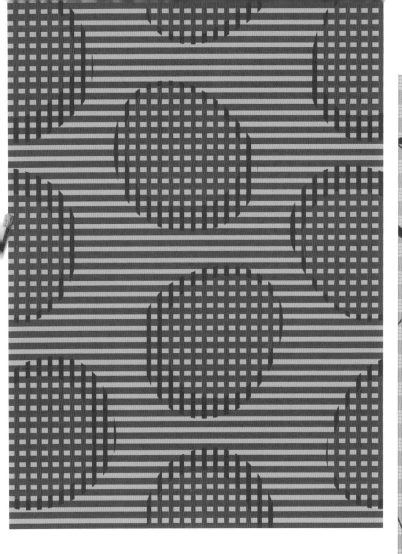

illustration (above left)
colour and patterns
exploration 2

illustration (above)
kampoeng daun 2

date
2006

date
2006

media/techniques
adobe photoshop

media/techniques
adobe photoshop

Amrita Sinha

I was born to an east Indian nuclear family with strong creative background. Most of my family pursue artistic interests. My father served in the defense ministry for 40 years and was posted to Madhya Pradesh in central India. I finished my schooling in a small city called Jabalpur where I was born. In those days pursuing a creative field like fashion or fine arts was not considered a smart choice for students. However, after fighting the opposition I applied for a Diploma in Fashion Design, at the National Institute of Fashion Technology in Chennai which is in southern India. I am presently living in Bangalore, Karnataka, working for the casualwear brand, Weekender.

I consider print as an art more than a craft simply for its diversified nature and adaptability: it can be worn, it can be displayed, it can be anywhere and everywhere.

Pop Art has been a source of inspiration. I particularly admired Andy Warhol and Jason Brooks's illustrations for the breakthrough use of colour and repetition and form to create pattern. I also love the earlier 20th-century art Art Nouveau. I love the shapes and silhouettes, and the off-beat nature of everything that was created during this era.

I respect Emilio Pucci for his impeccable sense of colour and Versace for his opulent and distinct style. My technique has lot of focus on the way the pattern repeats and I think it is retro with influences from the past.

When creating my own designs I start off with the motif in itself. I don't like the motif to be very complicated or too big – I prefer to work on the finer details of the motif and its delicateness, preferring line and hand-drawn technique. My personal preference for motifs is either geometric or floral. I like to create a repeat that complements the motif best and that gives the overall pattern its individuality. The repeat also gives it identity and usability. Having no repeat or having a very large repeat restricts the work to only certain types of surfaces.

illustration
polka rings

As a student I have loved paper, but as a professional I have been using computer applications like Corel Draw X3, Adobe Photoshop CS2 and Adobe Illustrator.

date
2007

I have visited textile fairs like Premier Vision in Paris that keeps the designer abreast of the latest global technological advances and breakthrough printing techniques and the design innovation.

media/techniques
corel draw/adobe photoshop

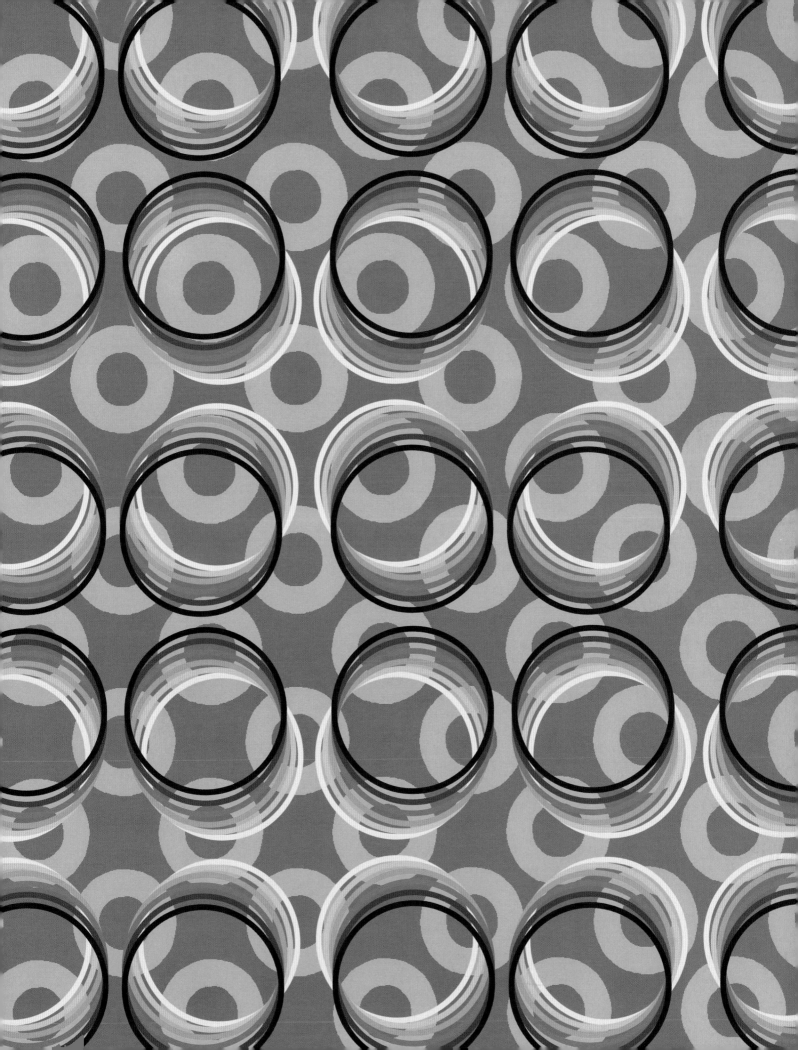

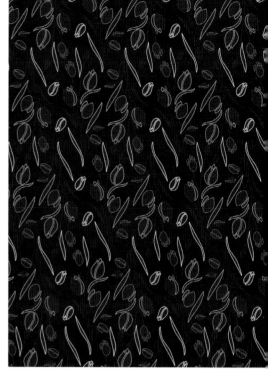

illustration (above)
digital flora

date
2007

media/techniques
adobe photoshop

illustration (above right)
tulips new 1

date
2006

media/techniques
corel draw/adobe photoshop

illustration (right)
nightbush

date
2006

media/techniques
corel draw/adobe photoshop

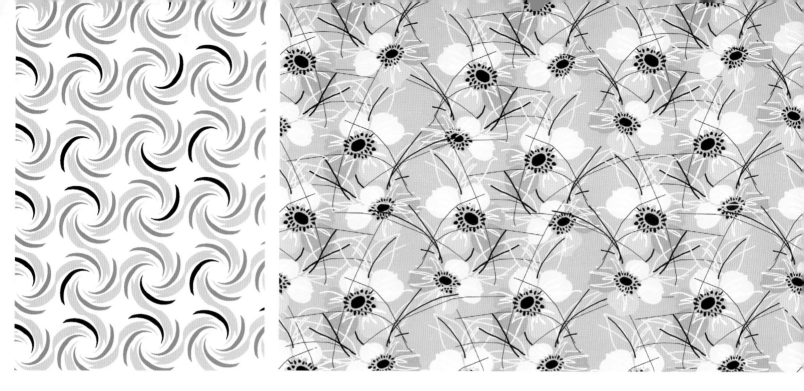

illustration (top left)	**illustration (above)**	**illustration (top right)**	**illustration (above)**
crazy ball	octachrome	fall bloom	beryl bloom
date	**date**	**date**	**date**
2004	2007	2004	2006
media/techniques	**media/techniques**	**media/techniques**	**media/techniques**
adobe photoshop	corel draw	adobe photoshop	corel draw/adobe photoshop

Yukari Sweeney

I was born and raised in Japan by my very traditional father, who made me learn calligraphy at a young age because he believed that handwriting shows our personality and upbringing. Later on in life, my rather liberal mother allowed me to explore the world without concern for what people thought about me. I think this was what spurred me on, without much planning or knowledge of the place, to move to England.

Being Japanese, I was, and still am, fascinated by what I suppose could be called 'Britishness'; the history of manor houses, the English countryside and hunting portraits always interested me in particular. My design and use of colour reflects this closely.

I always try to put an element of humour in my work, as I find taking yourself too seriously doesn't get you very far in life. Maintaining a sense of timelessness is important as well; I still remember the occasion when I was working for a fashion house in Japan. I was given the most beautiful Hermès scarf from my colleagues; and it still remains with me and gives me the same amount of joy today that it did those many years ago.

My reason for becoming a textile designer was mainly due to Eley Kishimoto; I found their design ethic inspiring and, as a student, I felt so lucky to have been given the chance to gain work experience in their studio. Apart from learning through their designs, I realized how much effort had to be put into actually making them a reality; even washing screens needed a lot of attention, otherwise the end product would be altered.

Through this work experience, I developed my own process of designing; for example, I prefer hand drawing all my designs because I see it as giving a more personal touch to my work. I use computers as a process to decide layouts and create repeats, then handprint onto fabrics.

illustration
afternoon tea

date
2006

media/techniques
adobe photoshop

I don't really think about the end product too much as I find it limits me; I believe there are plenty of clever people in the fashion industry that could make the most out of my prints. Having said that, I think that textile designers should inspire fashion designers and vice versa. After all, we're all in the same boat when it comes to creating fashion.

As a designer I think it's important to know about trends, but not be overtaken by them. I prefer people to have style, not to follow trends blindly, so I hope that such people would enjoy my designs.

186

illustration (above)
inside a gentleman's heart

date
2007

media/techniques
adobe photoshop

illustration (above right)
woodland treasure

date
2006

media/techniques
adobe photoshop

illustration (right)
hide and seek

date
2007

media/techniques
adobe photoshop

illustration (above)

wish you were here

date

2006

media/techniques

adobe photoshop

Index

Contact details

AMSTERSTAMPA
Email: amsterstampa@planet.n
Website: www.amsterstampa.com

LAURA-MARIA AROLA
Email : lauramaria.arola@googlemail.com
Website : www.lauramariaarola.com

ESTHER MIRO BRYANT-LINDSAY
Email : miro.textiles@gmail.com

CLAUDETTE CARINO
Email : claudettemcarino@yahoo.com

GIOVANNA CELLINI
Email: gio@giovannacellini.com
Website: www.giovannacellini.com

GEORGIA CHAPMAN
Email: info@vixenaustralia.com
Website: www.vixenaustralia.com

JILLIAN COLE
Email: jillian@jilliancoledesigns.co.uk
Website:
www.jilliancoledesigns.co.uk

ARTHUR DAVID
Email: arthurdavid@arthurdavid.ch
Website Address: www.arthurdavid.ch

AMANDA LE DONNE
Email: arledonne@gmail.com

LAUREN ENGLER
Email: lauren_engler@hotmail.com
Website: www.laurenengler.com

CATALINA ESTRADA
Email: catiestrada@gmail.com
Website: www.catalinaestrada.com

VICKI FONG
Email: vicki@vickifong.co.uk
Website: www.vickifong.co.uk

KAREN GENTILE
Email: karengentile@mac.com
Website: www.members.aol.com/artink1
or http://web.mac.com/karengentile

NADJA GIROD
Email: nadja@nadjagirod.com
Website: www.nadjagirod.com

SMRITI GUPTA
Email: smriti@studiosmriti.com
Website: www.studiosmriti.com

LAURA HOYER
Email: laura@openfacesandwich.com
Website: www.openfacesandwich.com

JULIE INGHAM
Email: julieingham@btconnect.com
Website: www.designbyjulieingham.co.uk

HOON JU KO
Email: folly96@gmail.com ,
info@pinkasparagus.com
Website: www.pinkasparagus.com

AMY VAN LUIJK
Email: avanluijk@gmail.com

JAMES FRANCIS MILLAR
Email: james@jamesfrancismillar.com
Website: www.jamesfrancismillar.com

KYUJIN LEE
Email: qjin70@yahoo.co.uk

JESSICA MICHELLE NADLER
Website: jessicamichellenadler.com

DAVINA NATHAN
Email: design@davinanathan.com
Website: www.davinanathan.com

RUPERT NEWMAN
Email: rupertnewman@hotmail.com
Website: www.rupertnewman.2day.ws

SAORI OKABE
Email: saoriokabe@hotmail.com

NATHALIE PELLON
Email: npellon@naklar.ch
Website: www.naklar.ch

LONGINA PHILLIPS DESIGNS
Email: lola@longinaphillips.com
Website:
www.longinaphillipsdesigns.com.au

Gina Pipét
Email: ginapipet1@hotmail.co.uk
Website: www.ginapipet.com

FAIZAL REZA
Email: skuirtgun@gmail.com
Website: www.skuirtgun.com

ALEX RUSSELL
Email: alex@alexrussell.com
Website: www.alexrussell.com

STEWART RUSSELL
Email: stewart@spacecraftaustralia.com
Website: www.spacecraftaustralia.com

YOSHIKO SAITO
Email: iam@yoshiko.co.uk
Website: www.yoshiko.co.uk

JANIS SALEK
Email: janissalek@verizon.net

SANDRA SETYAWAN
Email: sandrasetyawan@gmail.com
Website: www.sandrasetyawan.com

AMRITA SINHA
Email: amrita11680@yahoo.co.in
Website: www.coroflot.com/amritasinha

NIAMH SMITH
Email: niamhsmithzer@hotmail.com

REMY STEINER
Email: remy@botstyle.com
Website: www.botstyle.com

YUKARI SWEENEY
Email: yukari@yukarisweeneydesign.com
Website: www.yukarisweeneydesign.com

JAMAL 'BAM' TATE
Email: darkreign@mac.com
Website: www.darkreignstudio.com